ELDERLY WOMEN

ELDERLY WOMEN
Vulnerability and Support Structures

M.Z. Khan
Mohd. Yusuf
Archana Kaushik

GYAN

ISBN: 978-81-212-1187-1

Price: ₹ 785

First Published 2013

Published by

Gyan Publishing House
23, Main Ansari Road, Daryaganj,
New Delhi - 110002
Phones : 23282060, 23261060 Fax : (011) 23285914
E-mail: books@gyanbooks.com
website: gyanbooks.com

Laser Typesetting : Rajender Vashist, Delhi
Printed at : G. Print Process, Delhi

Cataloging in Publication Data--DK
Courtesy: D.K. Agencies (P) Ltd. <docinfo@dkagencies.com>

Khan, M. Z. (Mohammad Zahir), 1936-

Elderly women : vulnerability and support structures / M.Z. Khan, Mohd. Yusuf, Archana Kaushik.

p. cm.

Includes bibliographical references (p.) and index.

ISBN 9788121211871

1. Older women--India--Social conditions. 2. Older women--Health and hygiene--India. 3. Older women--Services for—India. I. Yusuf, Mohd. (Mohammad), joint author. II. Panda, Archana Kaushik, 1974-, joint author. III. Title.

DDC 305.260954 23

Contents

List of Tables

List of Diagrams

List of Case-History

Preface and Acknowledgements

Of late, the situation of elderly woemn has globally attracted the attention of the civil society. Not only do they tend to outnumber their male counterparts, but also their morbidity pattern, economic dependence and social situation entitle them to a concerted policy and programme attention. The situation of elderly women in India is no different. And added to this is the issue of vulnerability: There are a host of economic, cultural and social factors, which appear to accentuate their vulnerability, and which call for a proactive policy initiative.

India is a developing country. It has one-fourth of the population living below the poverty line (BPL) - and BPL varies from state to state. This gives rise to the question: What is the situation of elderly women in high BPL states? What is the social support system available to them at the familial and community levels? How do they cope? What have been the impact and reach of social assistance and welfare programmes evolved by the government and civil society organisations? What measures need to be taken to reduce vulnerability among elderly women? The present work is a modest attempt to find an answer to these and similar prickly questions, and to get at the complex and multi-dimensional issue of vulnerability among elderly women.

Feminisation of ageing is a worldwide phenomenon. Demographic projections show that the elderly females will far outnumber their male counterparts in the next few decades. In the decade 1991-2001, the population of elderly women in India has increased by 47 percent, as against 34 percent that of elderly men. The trend is also reinforced by the present study. The average age of the elderly women is found to be 67 years compared to that of the husbands' 70 years. Added to this, higher incidence of widowhood, illiteracy, malnutrition, and high economic dependency underscore the vulnerability of elderly females. On the other hand, literature survey brings out the insufficiency of the existing body of information on aged women in the country.

With the foregoing in view, the present study, has been conducted by HARYALI Centre for Research and Development, New Delhi, in collaboration with the Ministry of Women and Child Development, Government of India and the United Nations Development Programme (UNDP).

The study aspires to develop a dependable and comprehensive understanding of the phenomenon of vulnerability among elderly women, with a view to facilitating the formulation of appropriate policies and programmes having the ability to effectively curb and control the problems encountered by elderly women in their day to day living in low income states in India. As would be seen, the study has been able to build up a comprehensive data base on the status vulnerability and development needs to elderly women. It has been conducted in the states having a large proportion of BPL households, which include Assam, Bihar Chhattisgarh, Jharkhand, Madhya Pradesh, Odisha, Sikkim and Uttar Pradesh. Spread over 32 districts the study has gathered information from a large number of (numbering 7,766), their caregivers 5,743) and stakeholders (1,661). In addition, a large number of case studies and focus group discussions (FGDs) have been conducted.

Having analysed the risk factors, the study has attempted to develop a holistic view on economic, health and social vulnerability. Assessment of Economic Vulnerability brings out that about a fourth of elderly women are highly vulnerable.

Given the relatively large database and multi-faceted inform, the findings of the study may facilitate in evolving comprehensive and effective schemes to improve the social economic nutritional and health status of the elderly women in low-income states, particularly those living below the poverty line.

It must be put an record that carrying out the present work and bringing it to a satisfactory head have been poossible because of several intellectuals, professionals and researchers who have extended unflinching support and help. Space constraints do not allow acknowledging the contribution of all of them. However, a prominent few must be mentioned.

We are extremely grateful to Prof. K. Seeta Prabhu, Head, Human Resource Development Centre, UNDP, for providing the opportunity to conduct the study and for all the enlightened interest she has taken during the implementation of the study. She has offered several invaluable suggestions. Ms Meenakshi Kathel, Research Associate (Gender) and Ms Nishu Nirula, both from UNDP, have facilitated the work at different stages of its implementation (the reponsisbility of the views expressed in the report is of the authors alone).

Mrs Parul Debi Das, IAS, Joint Secretary and Mrs. R. Savitri, Director, in the Ministry of Women and Child Development, Government of India, have provided their valuable inputs during the formulation of tools of data collection and in the study as a whole. We are earnestly thankful to them and expect from them similar help and cooperation in the future too.

We extend our heartiest thanks to late Mr Mushtaq Ahmed, Former UNESCO Advisor to the Government of Nigeria and Zambia and Chairman of Core Group for Evaluation of Adult Education Programmes, Government of India, who has been a beacon at almost all the stages of the present work. As member of Research and Advisory Committee, he had provided guidance and encouragement throughout the conduct of the work.

We are equally indebted to Dr Ravendra Singh (Honorary Advisor, HARYALI), Director, National Commission on Population, Ministry of Health and Family Welfare, GOI, who has given us time and support in spite of his extremely busy schedule. His inputs have greatly helped and enriched the study in ways more than one.

We also thank our field team members who have diligently collected data under difficult conditions with enthusiasm and commitment. Without their hard work, this study would not have seen the light of the day. We also thank the office staff members at HARYALI-Centre for Rural Development, who have worked hard, especially during data coding, and often stretching beyond their working hours to meet the deadlines.

The present study would have been difficult to complete without the help and cooperation of the elderly women, their caregivers and stakeholders and many other persons who have facilitated data collection in numerous ways. We earnestly thank all of them.

Present work would not have seen the light of the day, Gyan Publishing House, New Delhi, not taken an enlightened interest in bringing it out in print. He has closely overseen the publication work at all its stages. We deeply appreciate his interest and commitment.

We do hope that the present work would provide much needed insight into understanding of vulnerability issues among elderly women, and help in reducing the conditions that pose hurdles to their well-being, and creating conducive environment in which elderly women would be able to live a life of contentment, fulfillment and dignity.

M.Z. Khan
Mohd. Yusuf
Archana Kaushik

1

Introduction

Growing population of the elderly is a welcome feature, as it denotes, among others, success story for public health policies as well as social and economic development. Worldwide, the proportion of the elderly people is growing faster than any other age group. Rapid and substantial advancements in nutrition, public health system and medical sciences have led to decrease in mortality rates and increase in life expectancy. This has resulted in what is popularly termed as population ageing, that is, an substantial increase in the proportion of the elderly in the general population. It was one of the most distinctive demographic features of the twentieth century and is continuing in the twenty-first century, too. Initially population ageing was experienced largely by developed countries, but recently it has become equally apparent in developing countries, too. Consequently, we are fast approaching a grey world. In the near future, virtually all the countries would be facing greying of population, though at varying rates.

While population ageing is often taken to be as one of the significant achievements of human civilisation, some economists and planners believe that greying of society is a drag on socio-economic change and development. This point of view of considering the elderly as a 'burden' rather than human resource, tends to make them even more vulnerable in society.

On the contrary, it is a fact that the elderly people in their prime of life have contributed, in myriad ways, to the growth and betterment of the society. Given this, society has an obligation towards them to stand by them, and provide them care, support and respect (see Khan, 1997). Are we giving our elderly their due love, respect and support?

Apart from the rise in absolute and relative numbers of aged persons in the population, several socio-cultural changes seem to have added to vulnerability of the elderly.

As is well-known, yester-years had a markedly different scenario. Agrarian society and joint family system used to be the dominant features in ancient and medieval times. These were no less than a boon to the elderly. The joint family system used to be a 'social safety net', for one and all, particularly for the aged people. The oldest male in the family would invariably head the family, wield much authority, and have a high status. This would lend respectability and status to the elderly persons. They would head the household, exercise almost total control over income and assets of the household as well as over family decision-making. The elderly used to be in the forefront of family and community affairs and decision-making. Besides, their knowledge and skills would be relevant to agricultural economy, and they would guide youngsters on sowing, irrigation, weeding, harvesting, etc. They would act as custodian of rituals and religious ceremonies. In many situations, the social institution of community or *biradari* had also evolved sanctions for the care of the elderly by the family, and acted as a pressure group in protecting their interests. Thus, they used to enjoy affection, respect, status, authority, and security in the family and the community.

The situation of elderly women was, however, a little different. It may well be kept in view that they were very much a part of the predominantly patriarchal system. Rarely did women have social status equal to that of men. During the *puranic* period, they gradually and imperceptibly lost most of their rights and came to have a subservient status and role. *Manusmriti* imposed several and highly restrictive conditions on women. They were discouraged from acquiring religious education. The role of a woman was confined to being daughter to her father, wife to her husband and mother to her children. The possibility to have an autonomous space was ruled out. She was expected to be dependant — socially, emotionally and financially— on the male family members, throughout her life.

Looking at the gender dimension, Sen (1994) points out, "... the roots of vulnerability in later life have, often, related to a life time of gender-based economic, social, and cultural inequalities where social roles combined with differential opportunity structures available to men and women have their effect". A woman was socialised and expected to internalise ideals of submissiveness, self-denial, self-effacement and self-sacrifice and devotion to husband. Emphasis was laid on how to be a 'good wife and daughter-in-law'. Her roles were confined to the four walls of the household. Active social engagement outside the house and interactions were openly discouraged.

It is important to note that elderly women, in ancient and medieval times, did enjoy some status and respect, though not at par with their male counterparts. Much of this could be attributed to the agrarian social structure and joint family system. As mother-in-law, a woman would exercise extensive authority over her daughter-in-law. She would have a major say in household matters. In fact, elderly women would have an important place in the power structure in the family. All this, however, would seldom override the factors that influenced socialisation process, moulding the personality of children in ways that perpetuate female subordination (see Panda, 2005). Needless to state, this kind of internalisation of gender inferiority substantially contributed, and continues to contribute, to the vulnerability of the elderly women.

In modern times, the situation has changed radically. Processes of commercialisation, urbanisation, and industrialisation, have brought about perceptive changes in the status of the elderly. Joint-family households, that were considered to be safe haven for the elderly, are giving way to nuclear family groups. The value system, too, has undergone rapid changes, and these changes do not always favour grey years. Likewise, rapid technological advancements and specialisation in the job market render skills of most elderly persons irrelevant, even redundant. Migration is another phenomenon that aggravates the situation of the elderly as, most often, children go out to distant places and aged parents are left alone. These factors have made the situation of the elderly highly vulnerable. How do the elderly cope with the new situation? What are the dimensions of vulnerability? What factors accentuate or reduce the vulnerability among the elderly? Does the patriarchal social structure contribute to vulnerability of the elderly?

It may be added that the situation of the elderly in the changing social scenario has evoked much concern, nationally and globally. Let us have a close look.

International and National Perspective

Globally, gerontologists have recognised the fact that the growing elderly population calls for a sensitive approach to protect and promote their interests. The United Nations, in 1982, organised the World Assembly on Ageing at Vienna. Among others, the forum evolved and launched an International Action Programme for the Aged.

The Action Programme aims at guaranteeing economic and social security to older persons as well as providing them with opportunities to contribute to national development. The Assembly sponsored the idea of 'active ageing' as an important strategy for adjustment of the aged in the society. Again, in 1991, the United Nations has laid down a set of five principles for ushering in an aged society — independence, participation, care, fulfillment and dignity of the older people. It implies that we are not only concerned with increasing the longevity, but also intend to 'add life to years'.

Subsequently, in the year 2002 the United Nations convened a second World Assembly on Ageing in Madrid, to review the progress and suggest a new plan of action. International Plan of Action on Ageing 2002 (India is signatory to this) aims on 'creating a society for all ages' by seeking commitment from all to ensure equal access to healthcare, nutrition, shelter, opportunities for economic independence, security and well-being. It also talks about ensuring gender perspective in all policies and programmes for the aged. Taking note of the increase in the population proportion of the elderly in the world, and in recognition of their rights, the Plan of Action has presented the world at large with a systematic approach to redefine and re-examine policies for promoting their well-being. What has been the impact of these steps at the macro level and on the ground realities, especially in relation to the vulnerability of elderly persons?

In view of the emerging challenges, the Government of India has formulated a National Policy for Older Persons, in 1999, an Action Plan, and National Council for Older Persons.

The National Policy on Older Persons abundantly reflects that the older persons' concerns are national concerns. It is based on the principles of financial security, healthcare and nutrition, shelter, education, welfare and research and training as main components for the well-being of the elderly.

Socio-demographic Scenario

Every year, around 9 million older persons are being added to the world's population. As a result, there is a new period after superannuation, often termed as 'third age'. It is projected that there may be, in the next 50 years, more grandparents than grandchildren, particularly in developed countries. In the next few decades, most rapidly ageing countries like Sweden, Japan, Germany and Italy will have 40 per cent or more elderly persons in their population (UNDP, 1999).

Table 1.1: Proportion of elderly persons in different regions and their age (in years)

Region	*Year*	*65 and above*	*75 and above*	*80 and above*
Europe	2000	15.5	6.6	3.3
	2015	18.7	8.8	5.2
	2030	24.3	11.8	7.1
North America	2000	12.6	6.0	3.3
	2015	14.9	6.4	3.9
	2030	20.3	9.4	5.4
Oceania	2000	10.2	4.4	2.3
	2015	12.4	5.2	3.1
	2030	16.3	7.5	4.4
Asia	2000	6.0	1.9	0.8
	2015	7.8	2.8	1.4
	2030	12.0	4.6	2.2
Latin America	2000	5.5	1.9	0.9
	2015	7.5	2.8	1.5
	2030	11.6	4.6	2.4

(contd...)

Region	*Year*	*65 and above*	*75 and above*	*80 and above*
North Africa	2000	4.3	1.4	0.6
	2015	5.3	1.9	0.9
	2030	8.1	2.8	1.3
Sub-Saharan Africa	2000	2.9	0.8	0.3
	2015	3.2	1.0	0.4
	2030	3.7	1.3	0.6

Table 1.1 brings out the proportion of elderly in the major regions of the world. It clearly shows that Europe is still the *oldest* world region, and Africa the youngest. The proportion of the elderly in the high growth populations of Africa, Asia and Latin America is still low, but a fairly sharp rise in the first two decades of the twenty-first century is anticipated. Except Africa, at least ten per cent of the populations in the developing regions would be of older persons by 2020.

Italy is now the world's oldest major country followed by Greece, Sweden, Spain and Japan (US Census Bureau, 2000). The phenomenon of ageing and the issues related to it are not essentially confined to developed countries alone. Over half (59 per cent or 249 million people) of the world's elderly live in developing nations and by the year 2030, 71 per cent (or 686 million) of the world's elderly would be living in developing nations. East and South-East Asia are fastest ageing regions.

Indian Situation

In this regard, India is no exception. With more than 1000 million population, after China, it is the most populous country in the world. Its elderly constitute the fastest growing segment of the population and is expected to cross 200 million by 2025. Demographic scenario in India shows a steep rise in the number and proportion of the elderly in the next few decades. The size of the elderly population has risen from 12.1 million in 1901 to approximately 77 million in Census 2001.By 2013, the number of elderly will rise to 100 million and by 2025 the number would be about 177 million elderly in the country. And in the next 25 years (that is, by 2050) this figure would be almost double (324 million). Added to this, majority (three-fourth) of the elderly people are in rural areas (Census, 2001).

According to the United Nations (1998) projections, the population of the aged in India is likely to be almost equal to that of Europe by the year 2020. During the twenty year period of 1980-2000, the aged population (60+) is believed to increase by 93.5 per cent in India, 78.8 per cent in Japan, 60.9 per cent in China and 57 per cent in the world as a whole (Guha Roy, 2002). The rate of growth of the elderly population would be higher than those of young and adult segments.

The United Nations (1999) has projected that much of the expected increase of the aged population in the twenty-first century will be in the developing countries, particularly, in China and India. It turns out that about 24 per cent and 15 per cent of the world's aged population will live in China and India at the end of the second decade of the current century.

Life-expectancy

An important indicator of ageing is the trend of average (further) duration of life in the old age range. National data trends show a modest but significant gain in longevity by the elderly over the decades. To exemplify, in India, at the time of Independence, expectancy of life at birth was just 32 years, female longevity being even less. Within a span of mere five decades, the demographic situation has markedly changed. The life expectancy at birth for females has been rising continuously and during 2002-06, it was 64.2 for females as against 62.6 years for males. Also, life expectancy is generally considerably high among urban people than among the rural ones as in 2002-06 it was 68.8 years in urban areas as against 62.1 years in the rural ones. Malaker and Guha Roy (1990) estimate life-expectancy, at 60 years of age, among males as 18.3 years, and among females as 20 years. Consistent with the world trends, female life expectancy is higher than that of males all through, though, at older ages, the difference is narrowing down. At 65 years, an Indian male has life-expectancy of 14.6 years, as compared to 15.9 in the case of females. At 75 years, corresponding figures are 7.5 years and 8.3 years, respectively, for men and women.

Gender Scenario

Further, the trend of feminisation of ageing is also clearly visible in developing nations. There would be 604 million elderly females in the World by the year 2025, of which 70 per cent would be in developing countries. Added to this, Africa and Asia have a high proportion of widows (De Alvarez, 1991). The situation of aged women in the South Asia is generally characterised by illiteracy, ignorance and poor health condition due to repeated and multiple pregnancies in their reproductive years. Much of it is attributed to patriarchal social structure that expects women to sacrifice their whole life for their husband and children and remain last in resource utilisation, be it nutrition, healthcare, education and participation. The first indicator of gender disparity in the country is sex-ratio.

Sex-Ratio: Skewed sex-ratio, in India, tells the story of existing prejudices and discriminations against females. According to the Census 2001, there are 933 females per 1000 males. Quite interestingly, after 60 years, women outnumber their male counterparts, though it is a recent trend (see Table 1.2). In 1901, sex ratio at ages 60 and above was 839 females per 1000 males.

In 1951, it was 973 and in 1961 there were almost equal numbers of elderly males and females in the country. After that, elderly women started outnumbering elderly men. In 1991, there were 1043 elderly women per 1000 males. This trend continued in 2001 also.

Marital Status: Looking into the marital status, the incidence of widowhood is much higher among aged females. Census 2001 brings out that 64 per cent of women and 19 per cent of men are widowed in the group of 60 years or more. At the age of 70 years and above, 80 per cent women and 27 per cent men experience widowhood. Higher life-expectancy for females at 60 plus and women marrying older men has resulted in large number of elderly widows. These demographic trends denote that ageing is, primarily, becoming an experience of females. In view of socio-cultural conditions, widowhood increases vulnerability of elderly women manifolds.

Literacy: For several reasons, illiteracy tends to increase vulnerability. Over the decades, India has attempted to

Table 1.2: Growth of elderly population by sex in India, 1901-2001.

Year	*Persons*		*Males*		*Females*	
	Number (in million)	*Percent*	*Number (in million)*	*Percent*	*Number (in million)*	*Percent*
1901	12.06	5.06	5.50	4.55	6.56	5.59
1911	13.17	5.22	6.18	4.81	6.99	5.65
1921	13.48	5.37	6.48	5.04	7.00	5.70
1931	14.21	5.09	6.49	4.86	7.27	5.35
1941	18.04	5.66	8.89	5.43	9.15	5.91
1951	19.61	5.43	9.67	5.21	9.94	5.66
1961	24.71	5.63	12.36	5.46	12.35	5.80
1971	32.70	5.97	16.87	5.94	15.83	5.99
1981	43.98	6.42	22.49	6.35	21.49	6.50
1991	55.30	6.55	28.23	6.45	27.07	6.66
2001	75.93	7.70	38.22	7.55	37.71	7.86
2011	95.92	8.1	48.86	8.05	47.06	8.23

Source: Ageing in India: Paper No. 2 of 1992: Registrar General and Census Commissioner, India; Report of the technical Group on Population Projection, 1996-2016 constituted by the Planning Commission, Registrar General, India, New Delhi, 1996.

eradicate illiteracy through planned efforts. As a result, successive decadal censuses have consistently shown an improvement in the literacy rates, though somewhat slow and sluggish. Census 2001 estimates literacy rate as 65.3 per cent as against 52.2 per cent in 1991.

Though literacy rate, in the country, is gradually increasing, educational status of the elderly is still unsatisfactory. In 1981, only about 35 per cent of the elderly males were literate as compared with 47 per cent of general male population. Among women the scenario is even worse. A quarter of the female population was literate in 1981, but only about 8 per cent of elderly women. Census 2001 shows that only 18.6 per cent of the elderly population is literate in the country with only 24.2 per cent males and 13 per cent elderly females are literate. What has been the impact of illiteracy on the vulnerability of the elderly?

Work Participation: It has been observed that the introduction of sophisticated technological advancements in economic pursuits, often makes the know-how of the aged less relevant. Added to this, compulsory retirement around 60 years aggravates the problems. Situation of aged females is much worse as they have, in general, remained housewife and economically dependent on their family. Viewing analytically, the work status of the elderly, data show that in 1991, in 60 plus age group, in urban areas, 42 per cent males and 5.4 per cent females were main workers whereas 57 per cent males and 94 per cent females were non-workers. Corresponding figures of elderly non-workers for rural areas were 35 per cent males and 81 per cent females, respectively. Census 2001 says that only 1.53 per cent males and 0.49 per cent females are main-workers. Statistics on the work participation of elderly are hardly encouraging, and may be contributing to their vulnerability.

Among the elderly, lower work participation rate has increased their dependency ratio (proportion of the population aged 60 and above to that of the working age population in the age group 15-59 years). Elderly dependency ratio has risen from 9.8 in 1951 to 12.3 in 1991. Another indicator called index of ageing expresses ratio of elderly (60 plus) to children (0-14 years) in the population (see Table 1.03). In 1951, it was 14.3

elderly per 100 children. In 1991, the corresponding figure rose to 18.4.

A sharp rise in the index of ageing, in 2001, disturbs many gerontologists as it indicates putting pressure on the working age group (15-59 years) and on the state, in meeting their basic and civic needs.

Table 1.3: Dependency ratios and indices of ageing in India, 1951-2001

Dependency Ratio				
Year	*Child*	*Elderly*	*Total*	*Index of ageing*
1951	68.49	9.80	78.29	14.31
1961	76.97	10.56	87.53	13.72
1971	80.82	11.47	92.29	14.20
1981	73.64	11.92	85.56	16.18
1991	61.43	11.31	72.75	18.42
2001	58.5	11.9	10.4	20.3
2011	44.9	12.8	57.7	28.6

Source: Sharma, S.P. (1994); Report of the technical Group on Population Projection, 1996-2016 constituted by the Planning Commission, Registrar General, India, New Delhi, 1996.

The demographic scenario gives us an indication of vulnerability of the elderly, particularly, of the women. The issues related to elderly would soon be relevant for almost all the families, communities and societies. The socio-economic and other age-related implications of population ageing go beyond demographic data, statistics and projections. Further, this demographic phenomenon poses unique challenges to every society. Let us try to understand various manifestations of vulnerability among the elderly.

Aging and Vulnerability

It is often assumed that advancing age imposes limitations on the elderly, adding to their vulnerability. It is, therefore, customary and convenient to see elderly persons as mere passive receptors of care. Since contemporary society values youth, preconceived notions about old age (irritability, amnesia, ill-health, etc.) are widespread. Often elderly people are taken as a burden or liability, incapable of contributing anything to the society. It is not rare to come across young people who regard old age as an incurable disease. Such myths often make ageing and the aged a subject of pity.

Looking from gender perspective, a woman is considered old when her son brings home the *bahu,* while a male on retirement is taken as old. As a result, women start facing prejudices and lowered status much earlier than their male counterparts.

More often than not, the society too has peculiar notions about the role and behaviour of the elderly subjecting them, directly or indirectly, to vulnerability. The age-old notion of dividing life into four *ashramas* — *bhramcharya ashram* (0 to 25 years of age, devoted to the acquisition of knowledge and skills), *ghrastha ashram* (25 to 50 years, associated with starting and enjoying family-life), *vanaprasthaashram* (50 to 75 years, start of detaching oneself from family and community) and *sanyasa ashram* (older than 75 years, denoted by complete renouncement from worldly affairs) — suggests that in old age a person shall not play an active or substantive role in family and community. This also reinforces the assertion that the society has certain preconceived notions about the passive role of the elderly. In order to have a deeper understanding of this issue, let us take a look at the vulnerability related to bio-psychological characteristics of old age.

Bio-psychological Aspects of Vulnerability

It would be interesting to note that there are nearly two lakhs centenarians in India. However, the image of a centenarian in mind is that of a frail, sick and dependent elderly. Though advances in medical sciences have provided with improved public health system, ageing itself brings many deteriorative changes in the body that are irreversible. Khan (1997) observes that in old age, there is a reduction in functional capacity of organs of the body, gradual tissue degradation, and cellular atrophy resulting in increased susceptibility to diseases and impairment of different body organs. With advancing age, due to physical deterioration and decrease in vitality, elderly people exhibit greater vulnerability to diseases.

Many ailments like arteriosclerosis, cerebro-vascular diseases, hypertension and diabetes are predominantly associated with age.

In old age, there is reduction in anabolic or 'building-up' reactions and increase in catabolic or 'breaking-down' reactions that mark deterioration in strength and body's functioning. Ageing also brings inevitable changes at the cellular, tissue and organic levels that lead to many deformities and diseases.

Weakening capacity of sensory organs leads to ailments like cataract, glaucoma, retinal disorders, hearing defects, denture, etc. As a consequence, the elderly lose independence in activities of daily living and become more prone to accidents and fractures. Respiratory diseases, such as chronic bronchitis and asthma disturb the elderly, particularly those in urban areas. Next, diseases like fibrosis, gout, rheumatism, arthritis, osteoporosis and spondalitis often pose locomotion problems among senior people. Also the sense of taste and smell diminish in old age, resulting in appetite loss and reduction in food consumption, which may further lead to many deficiency disorders. Also, the ageing body fails to supply enough oxygen to brain cells due to which there is increase in reaction time (Birren, et al., 1980). Such changes make the elderly introvert and rigid in their attitudes, impairing their social functioning. This demonstrates the inter-relationship between physiological and psychological changes. Such health problems also tend to influence the psychological well-being and social life of the elderly.

Ageing tend to increase mental morbidity, too. Depression and dementia often accompany ageing. Affective disorders, like paraphrenia and dementias (psycho-organic syndrome), form the bulk of total mental morbidity in the elderly. Rao and Mahadevan (1983) report that risk of psychiatric illnesses in the elderly increases with age. The overall prevalence rate of psychiatric morbidity increases 71.5 per cent for those over 60 years. Often, while physical impairments are recognised and treated, mental health problems go unnoticed.

Looking at the health status of aged women *per se*, we observe that they clearly are at a disadvantageous position than elderly males for many reasons. Apart from the age-related diseases, as mentioned earlier, they also suffer from gynecological problems. In Indian context, majority of women had early, repeated and multiple pregnancies. Lack of knowledge as well as resources for reproductive health, culture of silence discouraging any discussion on sexual matters with anybody, fear of stigma to access healthcare facilities and the like have contributed to their fading health in old age.

Moreover, their childhood, more often than not, is denoted by malnutrition, deficiency disorders and tendency of postponing treatment, which has a negative influence on their health in old age. Further, females are more prone to osteoporosis, particularly after menopause, which makes their bones quite fragile (Ganesh, 1997).

The elderly form a vulnerable group for multiple morbidities: physical, mental and social, among others. Let us look at some of the economic factors that increase vulnerability among the elderly.

Economic Aspects of Vulnerability

In most societies, superannuation from (paid) work marks the beginning of old age. More peculiar to males, the elderly retiring from the work often face social, emotional and economic crisis. There are, in India, hardly ten per cent of the elderly who have been in organised sector and receive retirement benefits. The other bloated category is of those in unorganised sectors, majority of them remain out of the pail of retirement benefits. Census 2001 estimates that there are 90 per cent of the elderly in unorganised sectors with no regular source of income. This change in economic position, when viewed in the context of current socio-cultural scenario, poses two daunting challenges. One, salable skills of the elderly are being outstripped by changing technology. Two, traditional sources of social security — family system and children — are fast losing validity both in rural as well as urban areas. These two conditions, if combined, push the elderly to the threshold of destitution.

Indeed, destitution or poverty is an objective reality in India. The data brought out by the National Sample Survey Organisation (1997) show that a third of the elderly in the country are below the poverty line. Further, another one-third of the aged are just above it. It signifies that the situation of nearly 66 per cent of older people is economically highly vulnerable. This group of elderly faces a lot of stress in making both ends meet. Lack of resources for subsistence often brings deteriorative age-related changes much faster among the elderly. It is often asserted that poverty puts elderly women into triple jeopardy — being poor, being aged and being female.

Needless to add, patriarchal social structure does not afford or allow adequate opportunity to women to acquire skills capable of providing economic independence. Studies show that they hardly enjoy property rights. This culturally notified dependence makes aged women rely on the male members of the family for the fulfillment of their economic needs.

In old age, the situation of women is generally precarious. Prakash (1996) argues that men who were once economically active are, in their old age, considered hapless and burden, what would be the situation of women whose work, more often than not, considered non-productive and who are mostly assigned the category of non-workers. This further adds to the economic vulnerability of aged women.

By way of social assistance, the society and government have initiated several measures to mitigate economic hardship of the elderly. In India, old age homes have been in existence for centuries. Of late, state governments and civic bodies have also set homes. Way back in 1969, Old Age Pension scheme was introduced in several states. Recently, government of India has introduced Bridh Yojna and Annapurna schemes. Have these initiatives been able to make a dent into the problem of economic vulnerability of the elderly? Do these make for a comprehensive safety-net for the elderly?

Socio-cultural Aspects of Vulnerability

Old age is the last phase of the life-cycle. The timing of this phase, its impact on roles and relationships, and the meaning attached to it, are determined by socio-cultural ethos. As discussed earlier, the life-span has changed considerably. As a consequence, steadily growing proportion of aged persons is unique feature of the present-day demographic scene. Telmon

(1988) observes that, paradoxically, there is an inverse relationship between the demographic weight of ageing people and their position in the society. In most societies when the number and proportion of the elderly people is low, they are respected, valued and honoured. However, when demographic phenomenon of 'population ageing' happens, due to its mounting burden on the younger earning population to meet rising cost of social security, it brings about a negative image of ageing.

In many developing societies, this conjecture may have ready acceptability. However, it may well be asked: Do the elderly make for a liability only?

In this regard, some kind of relationship between economic development and welfare, including that of the aged is emphasised upon. It is assumed that the former precedes the latter. In its support of this, the example is cited of developed countries that are able to offer a comprehensive social security system to senior citizens, while developing countries like India find it difficult to stand by older persons. In this, the point is often missed that many of the present-day developed countries were also developing countries, and in many of these countries, welfare, including elderly welfare has a history. The possibility is, thus, strong that welfare policies might have, directly or indirectly, contributed to or speeded up the pace of change and development in these countries.

At any rate, socio-cultural orientations appear to mould the way society looks at the elderly. This collective viewpoint does influence the vulnerability of the elderly population. Parsons (1960) observes that the extent to which old age is valued in a society depends on its dominant 'time orientation'. In 'past-oriented' societies, the aged are meaningful links to tradition and ensure historical continuity, especially with religious connotations. Our religious scriptures, among other teachings, also support ancestor worship. Contrarily, in societies with 'future-orientation' radical devaluation of old age is inherent, as is commonly observed in several modern and developed societies. Given these perspectives, let us look at the factors influencing vulnerability among the elderly, especially elderly women.

In view of contemporary social changes, due to modernisation, urbanisation, migration, increasing involvement of women in work force, widening intergenerational distance and decreasing family cohesiveness, care of the elderly is fast becoming a problem (Desai, 1983; Ramamurti and Jamuna, 1986; Ramamurti, et al., 1992b). Mishra (1996) observes that, since the knowledge and experience of the aged people are not considered necessary for the functioning of the rapidly changing new society, they are sidelined and their needs are neglected. If so, then, how do elderly women cope in a rapidly changing social environment?

Moreover, nuclear family set-up is becoming the order of the day for reasons more than one. It is said that urban areas characterised by high cost of living, limited living space, values like independence, privacy and consumerism are not able to accommodate and provide care and support to the elderly in the family. However, the situation in rural areas is no better either. More often than not, the young with their spouse and children migrate to urban destinations in search of economic opportunities, and their elderly parents are left behind in the village with their decreasing physical strength and lack of kinship support. Next, traditionally, the role of care-giving is assumed, more or less, by women. Now-a-days, women folk too are involved in economic activities outside home. Seldom do they have time even for domestic work, what to say of care-giving to the elderly. On the other hand, aged persons, particularly those who are 70-plus, need constant care. Financial stringency is yet another reason as to why middle and lower income-group families face problems in maintaining their elderly. Manifestations of vulnerability might vary, but they do exist cutting across rural-urban boundaries. A look into the gerontological literature at hand is likely to greatly facilitate a deeper understanding of vulnerability and its ramifications.

Literature Review

Over the years, the aged and their situation have attracted much scientific attention. So has been the case with the issue of vulnerability. This could well be looked into with a view to developing an insight into vulnerability and related issues and to finding out research gaps, if any. The present review of literature is divided into four inter-connected thematic issues.

(a) Nutrition and health and vulnerability: It goes without saying that nutritional needs of the elderly differ, and differ widely, from age-group to age-group, and from region to region. These also have something to do with gender. Gopalan et al. (1992) observe that the Indian elderly, especially the aged women, are at high risk of deficiency diseases due to chronic under-nutrition. Parbhu (1997) opines that gastric acidity decreases in large proportion of elderly persons, leading to impaired absorption of nutrients.

Khan (1997) reports that, in urban areas, 18 per cent of the elderly are assessed as ailing, 13 per cent as weak and rest as hale and hearty. Bhattacharya (1997) states that 85 per cent of people of over 65 years of age have at least one chronic illness and 30 per cent have three or more illnesses.

WHO report on Women, Ageing and Health (1998) brings out that people with higher education show less disability and have better chances of recovery after illness.

Gupta and Shankar (2006) maintain that older people usually suffer from chronic ailments. The duration of both acute and chronic conditions is longer for the elderly, and their chronic conditions are more likely to be lethal. They have listed that frequent chronic ailments among the elderly are diabetes mellitus, hypertension, cardiovascular diseases, cancer, arteriosclerosis, kidney diseases, Parkinson's disease, arthritis, dementia, etc. They further emphasise that these ailments are more severe in elderly women due to various economic and socio-cultural factors.

Paying attention to mental morbidities, Bose (2000) estimates that in India nearly four million elderly people are suffering from mental morbidity. This is a cause of serious concern, specially in view of woefully low psychiatric services. Similarly, Das (1994) reports that certain mental signs of old age are common among older people including loss in concentration or attention, loss of recent memory, development of religious sentiments, frustrations, depression, weakening of reflexes, etc. Bureau of Women's Welfare and Development

(1998) in its report, 'Women in India — A statistical profile', records that psychological disorders such as affective disorders, especially depression, dementia and delusional, are the major clinical symptoms among elderly widows.

Joshi and Sengupta (2000) observe that the elderly usually face a higher risk of developing mental as well as physical morbidity. Their vulnerability to mental health problems is due to ageing of the brain, physical problems, socio-economic factors, cerebral pathology, emotional attitude and the family structure. Feinson (1987) has found that older females have greater psychological impairment than their male counterparts.

On the level of anxiety, Khan (1997) reports that 61 per cent of elderly score low, 25 per cent average and four per cent high. Women are reported to have anxiety clearly more than men. About 41 per cent aged respondents are pessimistic, 38 per cent balanced and 22 per cent optimistic.

These studies do bring out that elderly suffer from many ailments and aged women in India are more susceptible to ailments and deteriorating health condition. This is equally true for mental morbidity. However, factors pertaining to vulnerability of elderly women with regard to nutritional and health requirements need to be further examined both in the context of rural and urban environment.

(b) Social conditions and vulnerability: Social support is regarded to be the biggest asset against vulnerability in old age. Interaction with family and 'significant others', involvement in community affairs, and respect from youngers bring a sense of acceptance and satisfaction among the aged (Stevens, 1992). Further, in the absence of family support, for one reason or the other, it would be or should be the duty of the community to look after them. Besides, community in terms of *biradari,* could exert considerable pressure on families to care for their elderly (Singh, 1995). Studying the situation of the elderly in rural Karnataka, Sivamurthy (2005) reports that, during crisis situations, 94.3 per cent elderly women from lower socio-economic strata received support from their family, whereas this proportion was only 75 per cent for those from upper socio-economic strata. Is it that social cohesion is relatively more in lower socio-economic strata?

Acceptance of the aged females in the family and community is critical for their well-being. It gives them a sense of self-worth. Assistance provided by social network helps the elderly deal more effectively with problems that confront them (Chadha, 1996; Krause, 1997). Sugisawa, et al., (1994) observe that social participation, social support and loneliness have indirect but very strong influence on the mortality of the Japanese elderly.

Similarly, Lin, et al. (1979) bring out that social support is inversely related to the incidence of psychiatric symptoms, and absence of social support is a better predictor of disorders than occurrence of stressful events. Ramamurti (1978) emphasizes that activities that do not involve other people are likely to fail as sources of satisfaction and well-being.

Rao (1994) observes that authority and status of the elderly have gone down in recent decades, and this is particularly true for rural communities. Their advice and opinion are not sought after as eagerly as was the case earlier. Often their views are considered obsolete. Further, the position of elderly females is noticeably vulnerable, mainly on account of patriarchal social structure. Study by Chadha, Willigen and Kedia (1996) shows that social involvement in old age substantially depends upon a number of factors including marital status, income level, individual resource control and health status. Individuals with poor health have significantly smaller social networks. For understandable reasons, widows have smaller social networks than the married ones.

Dhillon and Chhabra (1989) have studied psychosocial aspects. They lay stress on the differences in coping strategies of the elderly belonging to lower, middle and higher income groups, including interpersonal help, fatalism, escapism, action, optimism and control. Lopata (1978) is of the view that women experience greater stress on account of financial matters.

These studies provide an invaluable insight into the importance of social support for the aged women, and also the fact that a lack of social support has a perceptible and deleterious impact on females. However, socio-cultural specificities vis-à-vis social support to the elderly women needs to be studied in different social contexts. There is a pressing need for larger clarity on social issues that suppress or aggravate vulnerability.

(c) Economic condition and vulnerability: Economic insecurity is one of the crucial factors of vulnerability among the aged. In India, more than a fourth of the population is estimated to be living below the poverty line.

Khan (1997) observes that 16 per cent of the elderly, in economically poorer urban neighbourhood have such unmet needs as medical treatment, education, and marriage of their children. Panda (2005) reports that 93.4 per cent of the elderly women in Delhi had no income of their own in the prime of their life, while only 8 per cent of them were involved in some kind of the economically gainful work. Prakash (1989) pays attention to economic dependence independence among aged women. Only 17 per cent women have a share in their spouse's property.

Also, 90 per cent do not have any independent income or property. Chakraborty (2004) reports that majority of the retired elderly look for re-employment.

Is rural scene different or better in this regard? Muthayya (2004) observes that 31 per cent of the elderly in rural areas have no source of income. They could not meet expenses for want of money, including those on house construction, marriage of children, etc. Further, he observes that about 91 per cent lived in their own house — 55 per cent being just mud-houses.

The research studies discussed above clearly show economic dependence among the aged women. However, relationship between economic condition and vulnerability in various socio-cultural and economic settings needs further research attention.

(d) Social assistance measures for the elderly and vulnerability: Apparently, lack of knowledge about the existing schemes and programmes often increases vulnerability among the elderly. With low level of literacy and limited social engagements outside kinship make it difficult for elderly women to have updated information about schemes and programmes in existence for their own welfare. Khan (1997) takes a comprehensive view of the schemes and services for the elderly in two neighbourhoods of Delhi. He reports that only a fifth of the elderly have heard of the (OAP) scheme, among them 17 per cent feel that money given as OAP is very little and should be raised. Further, barely seven per cent of the elderly persons have heard of day care centres and none has ever availed the services. Similarly, awareness about old age homes was equally low: Only seven per cent of the elderly have heard about it.

Shah (2004) finds that 18 per cent of the elderly in rural areas find it difficult to access health services at primary health centres or sub-centres on account to inadequate transport facility to reach far-off health-care facilities. This is another dimension of inaccessibility of health care settings. Sasakumari (2001) finds that in Kerala almost 91 per cent are not getting any assistance from the government, about ten per cent of women are getting financial assistance in terms of old age pension/widow pension in urban areas and 9 per cent in rural areas.

These studies provide information about the problems surrounding the availability and accessibility of social assistance schemes, including lack of awareness among the elderly themselves. However, the situation in different cultural and regional settings needs to be systematically studied, along with the impact of these interventions in reducing vulnerability of the elderly women.

Critical Issues

The foregoing discussion brings out several facts concerning aged women, which need to be reiterated. There are at present more than 76 million elderly in India. As an offshoot, virtually every family is involved in providing care and support to the elderly. Furthermore, there are several challenges associated with the growing phenomenon of population ageing. Increased dependency ratio, rise in cost of social assistance and social insurance programmes, providing additional health care services, mental health programmes, helping the elderly to adjust to age-related physical, social and emotional changes, to mention a few.

Feminisation of ageing is a world-wide phenomenon. Demographic projections have it that the elderly females will far outnumber their male counterparts in the next few decades. Added to this, higher incidence of widowhood, illiteracy, malnutrition, high economic dependency project the vulnerability of elderly females.

Then, there is the issue of the elderly in the states in the country with high poverty line. The possibility cannot be ruled out that the elderly in these states face not only economic vulnerability but also a plethora of related psychosocial problems.

Literature survey highlights the insufficiency in the existing body of information on older women. In fact, research on the elderly, in India, is somewhat in a nascent stage. Moreover, aged women hardly get the attention of social researchers they should have. There is a need for a comprehensive database relating to various and diverse socio-cultural settings, focusing on the factors underlying vulnerability among the elderly women.

2

Research Methodology

Geriatric issues in recent decades have attracted much research attention. Yet, more attention needs to be devoted, on account of several cogent reasons. Improved nutrition, extension of primary healthcare to rural and tribal areas, advancements in medical technology, and upgradation of general health awareness have increased life expectancy and, thereby, brought about radical changes in the demographic structure — in most developed and developing countries. Unprecedented in nature, form and impact, these changes need to be properly analysed and understood.

The situation of the elderly women in India is somewhat unique. Socio-cultural factors that used to characterise the patriarchal society of yester-years persist even to this day. And these unmistakably weigh against the women, including elderly women. It is a common observation that sons are preferred over daughters, they have a larger share of household resources and, when of age, they dominate family decision-making. It is, thus, hardly surprising that most elderly women find themselves at the mercy of others, marginalised, or even excluded.

As is well known, in India, economic disparities are deep and wide. There are rich people and there are rich regions. The incidence of scarcity of resources, indigence or poverty differs, and differs widely from region to region. For welfare and development planning purposes, there is an officially declared 'poverty line'. It, too, markedly differs from state to state. There are states where only one household of every ten is estimated to be living below the poverty line (BPL), and there are others where four households are in this category. What is the situation of elderly women in high BPL states?

Then, we need to pay a concerted attention to rural areas. Nearly 70 per cent of the population in the country lives in villages. Needless to say, these do not have the kind of civic services that urban or metropolitan areas ordinarily have. So, is about the case with opportunity structures. Furthermore, official figures have it that indigence as indicated by BPL is clearly more in rural areas than in urban areas. Given this, there should be a comparative assessment of the vulnerability of the elderly women in rural and urban areas.

May it be noted that the elderly have to cope with age-related degenerative changes that affect physical and mental equipoise, which, in turn, tell upon their potential and capabilities, leading to a range of vulnerable situations. Many aged persons are given to withdrawal, alienation, loneliness, haplessness and hopelessness. This creates yet another source of the vulnerability. At any rate, dilemmas and difficulties of elderly women call for a thorough and systematic probe. This is what the present study is all about.

The study is based on the assumption that elderly women in the country, especially in low-income states, on account of several historical and contemporaneous reasons, are vulnerable. The study addresses the issue of vulnerability among the elderly women, particularly those in economically less-developed states both in rural and urban areas. Simultaneously, it plans to appraise household economic conditions as they are assumed to impact the well-being of the elderly. Side by side, the study plans to get at the civil society response as denoted by the social support system the elderly have in different states. These and similar considerations are the prime motivations behind the present study.

General Goal

The overall goal of the study is —

> To develop a dependable and comprehensive understanding of the phenomenon of vulnerability among the elderly women, with a view to facilitating

the formulation of appropriate policies and programmes having the ability to effectively curb and control the problems of elderly women in India.

Specific Objectives

The specific objectives of the study are as follows:

1. To assess the current social and economic status of the elderly women in India, particularly in less developed states;
2. To analyse the main improvements and ailments afflicting the elderly women as well as their nutritional status, general condition of physical health, access to medical care, expenses incurred, etc.;
3. To look into the nature and level of vulnerability of the elderly women in the household and the community, as also to examine the risk factors e.g. livelihood, nutrition, physical and mental health condition, access to rights, etc.;
4. To critically review existing governmental and non-governmental programmes/schemes available to the elderly women in terms of their design, budget allocations, delivery, reach and impact;
5. To assess the nature of participation of the elderly women in the welfare and development schemes both in rural and urban areas; and
6. To suggest ways and means to reduce risks of nutritional and health, economic and social vulnerability of the elderly women, paying due attention to the budgetary capacity of low income states.

Operational Definitions

Adhering to a descriptive research design, the study takes an elderly woman as a female who has completed the chronological age of 60 years or more.

Vulnerability is defined as the weakness or strength of the element at risk. And risk is taken as the probability of harmful consequences, or expected loss of lives, people injured, property, livelihoods, economic activity disrupted (or environment damaged) resulting from interactions between natural or human-induced hazards and vulnerable conditions. Risk is conventionally expressed by the equation as: risk = hazard x vulnerability (UNDP, 1996).

Vulnerability refers to the risk of being in problems / difficulties on certain contingent conditions that require support system other than those available. These contingency conditions could be poor health, stringent economic condition, lack of sufficient means to handle crisis and limited social support system. In the case of elderly women in India, certain conditions that increase their vulnerability could be lack of sufficient means of livelihood, no ownership of movable-immovable assets, no/unwilling family members or other relatives, widowhood, abuse by family members, poverty, unemployment of self or any other family member, illiteracy, poor health condition, dependence in activities of daily living like eating, bathing, walking, small household chores, and so on, going down of sensory capabilities, locomotion, etc. This apart, patriarchal social structure has led to collective prejudices against women's equality and empowerment. This includes aged women themselves.

Various manifestations of vulnerability vis-à-vis elderly women could be:

- Advancing age itself can become a factor in enhancing vulnerability if it is accompanied by associated factors that force a person to change her preferred life-style and autonomy.
- Inadequate food intake due to poverty, lack of resources, abuse by caregiver, requirement of special diet and non-availability of the same, lack of knowledge about balanced diet, etc. This factor of vulnerability leads to poor health condition, which may, in turn, hamper the aged lady's well-being in several ways.
- Poor health condition, ailments like high/low blood pressure, diabetes, digestive upsets, breathing problems, and so on decreasing sensory capabilities like vision, hearing etc., often make the aged women vulnerable as these factors limit her autonomy in maintaining her preferred life-style.

- Certain social factors also hamper access to resources in the community. These factors can be belonging to a particular religion/caste/class or ethnic group.
- Widowhood in a patriarchal social structure does aggravate a woman's vulnerability as her identity is more or less governed by her husband. Societal perception becomes harsh towards her when she is without the 'support' of her husband.
- Patriarchal social structure has discouraged a woman to actively participate in community events and join formal social groups. As a result, majority of women have remained dependent on their family members for support and lack even information about these resources.
- Lack of knowledge about existing services and programmes is a major factor that can enhance vulnerability of an elderly woman.
- All factors that contribute to mental health problems like worry and tension, depression; loneliness, and the like, tend to enhance vulnerability of aged women.
- Elderly abuse, be it physical, social, emotional, verbal or mental, at the familial and/or community level increases vulnerability.

For the purpose of the present study, vulnerability may be defined as those contingent conditions that hamper the well-being (social functioning) of an elderly woman and requires the support system other than the existing ones to mitigate the factors that may result in helplessness and hopelessness, if not encountered promptly.

Needless to mention, **forms of vulnerability** are many, and vary from one cultural setting to another. The present study, however, focuses on the following five prominent forms of vulnerability of elderly women:

- **Nutritional vulnerability:** Vulnerability arising out of non-availability/denial of balanced nutrition required by an elderly man or woman thereby hampering her health.
- **Health vulnerability:** Vulnerability because of decreasing sensory capability, body strength, suffering

from ailments like high/low blood pressure, diabetes, digestive upsets, breathing problems, etc., that hamper an aged female's autonomy in activities of daily living.

- **Economic vulnerability:** Vulnerability due to lack of sufficient means of livelihood and other support systems that result in holding up of necessary expenditure and lead to economic insecurity.
- **Social vulnerability:** It is vulnerability resulting in changes in the social status at family and community levels manifested through abuse (physical, mental, verbal, etc.), and lack of or denial of opportunities of performing meaningful roles in the family like in decision-making, sharing household responsibility and reduced opportunities of meaningful interactions and congruent relationships with significant others.
- **Overall vulnerability:** Overall vulnerability is a composite variable of the above four variables (nutritional vulnerability + health vulnerability + economic vulnerability + social vulnerability).

Coverage of the Study

Universe: Women aged 60 years or more living in a family set-up and their caregivers constitute the universe of the study. However, women living alone in a non-institutional setting have also been included. Elected representatives of *panchayats*, NGO workers, Mahila Mandal members, District Social Welfare officers, Block Development Officers and health functionarie officials concerned with the implementation of various schemes like Old Age Pension, Annapurna, Day Care Centres, Old age Homes, etc., have been included in the category of stakeholders.

Selection of States: The study intends to look at the dimensions of vulnerability among elderly women in economically less developed states in India. Therefore, all the states have been arranged according to the proportion of households living below the poverty line (BPL), and eight states with high BPL have been selected. Table 2.1 below shows the selected states based on the BPL population:

Table 2.1: BPL Population in the selected states (1999-2000)

Sl. No.	*States*	*Percentage*
1	Assam	36.09
2	Bihar	42.60
3	Chhattisgarh*	37.87
4	Jharkhand*	42.60
5	Madhya Pradesh	37.87
6	Orissa	47.15
7	Sikkim	36.55
8	Uttar Pradesh	31.15
	All India	**26.10**

Source: Handbook on Social Welfare Statistics, 2004, Ministry of SJE, GOI.

*Assumed figures.

Assam and Sikkim have been selected from north-east because they have large number of BPL population as compared with other northeastern states. Bihar, Madhya Pradesh, Orissa and Uttar Pradesh also have large number of BPL component as compared with other states. Jharkhand and Chhattisgarh have been selected because they are newly created and taken as relatively less developed states.

Selection of Districts: Districts in the selected states have been then grouped geographically into four zones i.e. North, South, East and West. One district from each zone has been randomly selected (total number of districts selected is 32).

Selection of Urban and Rural Areas: Approaching the district headquarters, list of blocks/towns and villages/wards was procured. From each district, two development blocks (for covering rural area) and two towns (for covering urban area) have been randomly picked up. Subsequently, four villages from each block and two wards from each town from representative geographical regions have been randomly selected.

Selection of Respondents: For this purpose, voters list has been relied upon. It was procured either from the BDO

Office or from counselors or ward members in the concerned town / city. The sampling design required a sample of 20 elderly women from each location. However, a provision has to be made for 'casualties'. As such, 30 aged women have been randomly selected from each location, using Random Number Table. Details of sample households are given in Table 2.2.

About 11,520 households having elderly women were included in study sample. The eldest woman from each selected household was to be interviewed. In turn, from each selected household, the eldest male, termed caregiver in the study, was included in the sample (projected number, 11,520). Similarly, from each selected district 50 stakeholders (total number, 1600) were targeted for contact and information gathering.

At least one focus group discussion (FGD) in rural areas and one in urban area in each selected district were organised. Travel expenses and snacks were to be provided to the participants. Probable participants included the following:

- Concerned Government Officials (Social Welfare, DRDA, DUDA, etc.)
- Medical Persons (Govt. Doctors, Private Doctors, ANMs, MPWs, etc.)
- Representative of Civil Society (NGOs, Mahila Mandals, Panchayats, SHGs, etc.)
- Around 10 elderly women including men/husbands and their children from different communities

Tools of Data Collection

The study in hand is not only empirical but also a major research enterprise. To fulfill its enunciated objectives, it heavily draws upon both primary and secondary data. The latter are to be collected from a diverse range of sources, including —

- Census, NSSO and other official data
- Schemes/programmes of Government and non-government organisations at national and state level for the elderly women
- Available research studies, progress and evaluation reports of the schemes and related documents

Table 2.2: Targeted Sample of Households

State	*No. of Districts*	*No. of Blocks*	*No. of Towns*	*No. of Villages*	*No. of Wards*	*Total Households*		
						Rural	*Urban*	*Total*
Assam	4	8	8	32	16	960	480	1440
Bihar	4	8	8	32	16	960	480	1440
Chhattisgarh	4	8	8	32	16	960	480	1440
Jharkhand	4	8	8	32	16	960	480	1440
Madhya Pradesh	4	8	8	32	16	960	480	1440
Orissa	4	8	8	32	16	960	480	1440
Sikkim	4	8	8	32	16	960	480	1440
Uttar Pradesh	4	8	8	32	16	960	480	1440
Total	**32**	**64**	**64**	**256**	**128**	**7680**	**3840**	**11520**

For secondary or official data, suitable Proforma have been developed and multiple copies have been prepared for the use of the research team.

As discussed earlier, primary data were to be collected from elderly women, elderly men/their husband, their care-givers and stakeholders. What would be the most suitable method of information-gathering? The study was to be implemented in low-income states, and the possibility cannot be ruled out that these would also be low on literacy and education. It ruled out the use of 'mail-questionnaire'. Would observation technique be suitable for present purposes? For several reasons neither participant observation nor non-participant observation was feasible. Moreover, these techniques are very time-consuming.

As discussed in Chapter One, the present study intended to delve into several subtle dimensions pertaining to the lifestyle and problems of the elderly women. This called for rapport, even transference, between researcher and the subject. Given this, interview technique becomes the obvious choice for gathering information from the elderly women, their care-givers and stakeholders. Interview-setting allowed for face-to-face contact, non-verbal communication, rapport-building, and probe or follow-through queries. It had scope to properly and effectively handle 'emotional' or 'crisis' situations.

Keeping these considerations in view, it had been planned to use interview technique with the three categories of informants, namely, elderly women, their care-givers, and stake-holders. Further, in order to have uniformity, comparability and scope for generalisation, the present study had opted for 'structured interview' technique.

In the light of the study objectives and the key issues arising from them, an interview schedule for elderly women has been drafted, covering such dimensions as identifying information, family background, economic condition, nutritional and health and well-being, accessibility to healthcare facilities, awareness and availability of social support system. The draft has been thoroughly edited and reviewed by several experienced researchers. It was translated into Hindi. Subsequently, it was been pre-tested on 50 aged women in Zakir Nagar, New Delhi.

In the light of pre-testing, the interview schedule, both Hindi and English versions, were modified in terms of contents, thrust and communication. Next, the schedules were rendered into Assamese, Gorkhali and Oriya languages. Further, it was planned that interview would be conducted in vernacular, but the responses would be recorded by the interviewer in English (on English-version schedule). Given this, the required number of copies of the interview schedule (English-version) were got printed.

To summarize, following tools have been developed and used in the study:

1. Interview schedule for elderly women
2. Interview Schedule for care-givers (husband, son, daughter, etc.)
3. Interview schedule for the stakeholders (representatives of civil society and government officials)
4. Check-list for the agencies implementing various schemes for the aged
5. Check-list for review of the programmes/schemes
6. Check-list for the Case Study
7. Guideline for Focus Group Discussion (FGD)

Data Collection

As is evident,the present study has relied upon both secondary and primary data. Secondary data have been gathered from libraries in Delhi, mainly from Indian Council of Social Science Research, Jawaharlal Nehru University, Jamia Millia Islamia University, National Council of Educational Research and Training, Delhi University, Help Age India, Age-Care India, etc. Also, information has been gathered from various ministries and government departments. Collecting census data, especially that of Census 2001, has been a tedious job. Many visits have been paid to different Census offices in Delhi. Added to this, data through the Internet have also been downloaded. However, gathering secondary data has been relatively an easy task as compared to primary data.

Both government and non-government agencies implementing development schemes / programmes for elderly women and men in sampled locations have been identified. Researchers have held detailed discussion with the concerned officials to ascertain their role in delivery, opinion about the advantage and disadvantages of the schemes, problems faced by them, and the participation of elderly women. Relevant related documents and reports on the schemes have also been collected for analysis and study back in Delhi. Likewise, the impact of these schemes on the beneficiaries has been assessed on the basis of progress and evaluation reports.

As planned,65 focus group discussions (FGDs) have been organised, both in villages and in towns. In many of these FGDs, high-ranking district officials (i.e. Additional Collector / Deputy Commissioners) have participated, and provided rich and varied information.

Conducting interviews has been a time-consuming but insight-giving work. While Table 2.02 outlines targeted interviews, Table 2.3 provides detailed information on those completed — according to state, district and sample.

Data Analysis

As would be expected, the study has generated a large body of information, both official and first-hand. Handling of official or secondary data has been relative easy: Sort and collate information and present it using statistical table, graphs or diagrams. Handling of first-hand or primary data, however, has been a different matter.

Codebook and tabulation plan were developed at the planning stage. When the work of data collection commenced, completed or filled schedules were simultaneously checked and rechecked for any errors and inconsistencies. As schedules also had open-ended questions, these coded as per specification in the codebooks. Subsequently, the data have been entered into computer on SPSS spread-sheet. Needless to mention, the data set is quite large: Interviews have originally generated 194 variables relating to the elderly women, 50 variables relating to care-givers, and another 50 variables relating to stakeholders.

This data set has been processed using such software as SPSS, Harvard Graphic and Microsoft Excel. One-way or

Table 2.3: Sample/Data Collection Completed

Sl. No.	*State / District*	*No. of Respondents*				*Case Studies & FGDs*	
		Elderly Women	*Caregivers*	*Stakeholders*	*Total No.*	*Case Studies*	*FGDs*
1.	**Assam**						
	1 Goalpara	247	224	33	504	3	2
	2 Kachar	261	235	26	522	4	2
	3 Sonitpur	235	185	38	458	6	2
	4 Tinsukia	235	209	27	471	5	2
	Sub Total	**978**	**853**	**124**	**1955**	**18**	**8**
2.	**Bihar**						
	5 Kathihar	236	175	42	453	2	2
	6 Madhubani	234	196	68	498	4	2
	7 Nawada	230	174	43	447	2	2
	8 Saran	243	187	64	494	2	1
	Sub Total	**943**	**732**	**217**	**1892**	**10**	**7**
3.	**Chhattisgarh**						
	9 Dhamtri	251	145	27	423	0	3
	10 Kabirdham	238	134	51	423	0	1

Sl.	State / District	No. of Respondents				Case Studies & FGDs	
No.		Elderly Women	Caregivers	Stakeholders	Total No.	Case Studies	FGDs
	11 Koria	243	128	48	419	1	2
	12 Raigarh	219	131	53	403	3	6
	Sub Total	**951**	**538**	**179**	**1668**	**4**	**12**
4.	**Jharkhand**						
	13 Dumka	240	200	51	491	6	2
	14 Garhwa	246	196	76	518	5	2
	15 Hazaribag	239	192	66	497	7	2
	16 West Singhbhum	269	177	32	478	4	1
	Sub Total	**994**	**765**	**225**	**1984**	**22**	**7**
5.	**Madhya Pradesh**						
	17 Betul	242	178	52	472	4	2
	18 Gwalior	243	206	44	493	3	2
	19 Indore	234	164	57	455	4	2
	20 Umaria	239	181	61	481	4	2
	Sub Total	**958**	**729**	**214**	**1901**	**15**	**8**

Sl. No.	*State / District*	*No. of Respondents*				*Case Studies & FGDs*	
		Elderly Women	*Caregivers*	*Stakeholders*	*Total No.*	*Case Studies*	*FGDs*
6.	**Orissa**						
	21 Bolangir	243	131	41	415	1	0
	22 Cuttack	250	178	35	463	4	3
	23 Ganjam	245	150	44	439	3	3
	24 Sundargarh	243	187	40	470	0	0
	Sub Total	**981**	**646**	**160**	**1787**	**8**	**6**
7.	**Sikkim**						
	25 East District	237	177	76	490	5	3
	26 North District	200	129	51	380	3	3
	27 South District	236	153	79	468	3	1
	28 West District	242	149	78	469	3	3
	Sub Total	**915**	**608**	**284**	**1807**	**14**	**10**
8.	**Uttar Pradesh**						
	29 Aligarh	323	291	32	646	2	0
	30 Barielly	243	222	28	493	3	1
	31 Gorakhpur	236	222	155	613	2	2
	32 Jhansi	244	137	43	424	3	4
	Sub Total	**1046**	**872**	**258**	**2176**	**10**	**7**

frequency tables have been prepared. This has been followed by the process of 'recoding', wherever necessary. Inter-linkages have been examined through two-way and three-way cross-tables — paying due attention to significance and relevance. Throughout, suitable statistical techniques and tests have been applied. Apart from proportion and percentage, these tests include mean, standard deviation, chi-square, product-moment correlation, rank-correlation, etc. Apart from statistical tables, presentation graphs and diagrams have been prepared. The computer data file, thus, developed has been subjected to usual accuracy and quality checks. The analysis based on primary data/information has been validated with secondary information.

In order to have a generalised and holistic view, the responses of elderly women gathered during the interview have been indexed and, following *scalogram* technique, composite variables of (a) Health Vulnerability, (b) Economic Vulnerability, (c) Social Vulnerability, and (d) Overall Vulnerability have been developed. Methodological and related particulars are discussed wherever these variables appear first in the report.

By way of qualitative analysis, a large number of insight-stimulating 'case studies' and 'best practices' have been compiled, utilising both quantitative and qualitative material, including 'observations of the interviewer'. These focalise both rural and urban areas pertaining to almost all the selected districts.

Research Report

In the light of study objectives, primary and secondary data, their analyses and interpretation, have been organised, and a report has been documented. At the planning stage itself, a detailed chapter scheme was prepared. This has been modified at the successive stages of the implementation of the study. This has greatly helped in keeping the work focused and directional.

In interpreting the data as well as in the writing work, a conscious effort has been made to maintain the point of view of elderly women. Likewise, due thought has been given to present findings in a way to provide an interface with policy framework.

The report is spread over nine sections. Chapter I deals with geriatric issues, situation of the elderly women and articulation of the research argument. Chapter II outlines the research methodology used to carry out the study. Chapter III analyses the socio-demographic aspects of ageing. Economic condition of the elderly women and of the household they live has been examined in Chapter IV. Chapter V critically looks into the state of nutrition and health of the aged women. To the elderly, social environment as defined by the web of interpersonal relations is equally important. These have been analysed in Chapter VI. For the support of senior citizens, there exist policy- and legal framework. Besides, there are several programmes and schemes. What is the level of their adequacy? What is their reach? These dimensions have been outlined and appraised in Chapter VII. Chapter VIII dwells on the conceptual and empirical aspects of 'vulnerability' among the elderly women. It also presents the quantification of vulnerability and its main components. The last section, Chapter IX is conclusion; and it recapitulates research issues, summarizes main findings, and makes a set of data-based recommendations.

Hopefully, the present work manages to shed a new and incisive light on the situation of elderly women in low-income states in the country; its findings would have an interface with the present and future social policy framework; and these would pave the way for more effective intervention programme for the benefit of elderly women.

3

Socio-Demographic Background

In modern times, population ageing is often taken to be a landmark in the history of human civilisation. It represents a confluence of lowered fertility, improved nutrition, and effective healthcare. These have contributed to longevity, resulting in growing number and proportion of older population, almost throughout the world. In most nations, there have been major reductions in the prevalence of infectious and parasitic diseases, declines in infant and maternal mortality, and improved nutrition. With all these socio-economic changes, more and more people tend to live long to mature old age. After the year 2010, the number and proportion of elderly, especially the oldest old, is projected to rise rapidly in most developed and in many developing countries. Demographically, most developed nations are among the oldest in the world today. In fact some of them may have more grandparents than children by the middle of the twenty-first century.

The United Nations (1999) projects that, by the year 2025, a major share (72 per cent) of the elderly population would be residing in developing countries. These developing countries are, often, characterised by poor economic conditions, lack of adequate healthcare, education and social welfare systems. For these countries maintaining elderly population would be difficult as there are hardly enough resources to meet the needs even of its younger population.And the cost of social insurance and social assistance for senior citizens can be quite taxing for nations with scarce resources.

Another important demographic fact that attracts the attention of gerontologists and social researchers is — 'ageing is feminised'. Globally, elderly women are outnumbering their male counterparts. The situation of elderly females, in developing nations, provides a discouraging picture. Illiteracy, poverty, social and economic dependency deprive elderly women of the skills and personal resources to cope with the changing physical, social and economic conditions. India is no exception to this.

Attention may be paid to the socio-demographic scene in India. Census 1991 had brought out that the population, in the age group of 0 -14 years, was 36.77 per cent, while the elderly population was 6.16 per cent. In 2001, the proportion of children, in the total population, has fallen to 35.4 per cent and the proportion of the elderly has gone up to 7.2 per cent. Demographers further predict that, by the middle of the present century, children (0 -14 years) would be about the smallest category in the Indian population (Vijayanunni, 1997).

Table 3.1 gives an overview of elderly population from 1901 to 2001 as well as decadal growth rates. It indicates that decadal growth rate among the elderly in 2001 has been more than four times its value in 1911. It may be noted that the proportion of female population among elderly is decreasing consistently over the decades which is contrary to the fact that worldwide trend of feminisation of ageing is being observed. This indicates vulnerability of elderly women in the country.

India represents wide diversities in terms of religion, caste, language, culture, per capita income, health, educational and nutritional status and other socio-cultural attributes. Also, the needs and problems of the aged differ from state to state. Moreover, social welfare schemes like Old Age Pension vary in different states. Many states face budgetary difficulties in providing for the aged population. It is therefore important to have a close look at some of the prominent socio-demographic factors that influence the well-being of eldrerly women brought under the focus in the study.

It may be restated that the states included in the study are Assam, Bihar, Chhattisgarh, Jharkhand, Madhya Pradesh,

Table 3.1: Population and Decadal Growth of Older Persons in India

Year	*Old Age Population*					*Decadal Growth Rate (%)*					
	Male		*Female*		*Total*	*Male*		*Female*		*Total*	
	No.	*%*	*No.*	*%*		*60+*	*All Ages*	*60+*	*All Ages*	*60+*	*All Ages*
1901	5501791	46%	6558055	54%	12059846	N.A.	N.A.	N.A.	N.A.	N.A.	N.A.
1911	6181329	47%	6987458	53%	13168787	12	6	7	5	9	6
1921	6482389	48%	7002375	52%	13484764	5	0	0	1	2	0
1931	6944128	49%	7264263	51%	14208391	7	11	4	11	5	11
1941	8890700	49%	9149300	51%	18040000	28	15	26	14	27	14
1951	9671048	49%	9941222	51%	19612270	9	13	9	13	9	13
1961	12356687	50%	12355422	50%	24712109	28	22	24	21	26	22
1971	16874325	52%	15825406	48%	32699731	37	26	28	24	32	25
1981	22022869	51%	21144519	49%	43167388	31	24	34	25	32	25
1991	29363725	52%	27317915	48%	56681640	33	24	29	23	31	24
2001	39268889	49%	40091904	51%	79360793	34		47		40	

Source: Ministry of Social JusticeandEmpowerment, Govt. of India, New Delhi.

Orissa, Sikkim and Uttar Pradesh. Table 3.2 presents relevant information about the elderly. In terms of number of elderly population, Uttar Pradesh tops the list, followed by Bihar and Madhya Pradesh. Sikkim has lowest number of elderly persons. Looking at gender distribution among elderly population, Orissa and Jharkhand have equal proportion of elderly males and females. Chhattisgarh remains the only exception where feminisation of elderly population is clearly visible. The reason for this trend in Chhattisgarh may be attributed to high concentration of tribal population in the state, where patriarchy does not hold its roots strongly.

A brief and comparative view of the study states on some important demographic and development indicators would be in order.

Assam: It has a population of about 266 lakhs as per the Census 2001. This northeastern state is predominantly rural, with just 12.7 per cent of urban population. It has literacy rate of 64.28 per cent, with 71.93 per cent literate males and 56.03 per cent literate females. Work participation rate in the state is merely 35.88 per cent, which includes 49.93 per cent males and 20.80 females. It is among the states with highest number of indigent persons — 36.09 per cent of the population in the state lives below poverty line. The state has fourteenth place on HDI or Human Development Index (dimensions: education, economy and health),

Bihar: It has a total population of 828 lakhs. Bihar is mainly rural and barely 10.5 per cent of its population lives in urban areas. It has literacy rate much below the national average: It is 47.53 per cent, with 60.32 per cent male and 33.57 per cent female literacy rates. Again, work participation rate is among the lowest in the country, that is, 33.88 per cent. Gender disparity is quite pronounced, work participation rate among males is 47.73 per cent, as against 18.84 per cent among females. Another socio-demographic indicator showing the dismal state of affairs in Bihar is the proportion of population living below the poverty line, it is 42.6 per cent, next to Orissa. Bihar occupies the fifteenth place on HDI.

Chhattisgarh: It is a newly constituted state with a total population of 208 lakhs, as per Census 2001. The state has

Table 3.2: State-wise Population of Old Age Persons – 2001.

Sl. No.	*Name of State*	*Total Population (All Ages)*	*Population of Aged Persons*					
			Total		*Male*		*Female*	
			No.	*%*	*No.*	*%*	*No.*	*%*
1.	Assam	26655528	1589340	6.0%	817793	51%	771547	49%
2.	Bihar	82998509	5679099	6.8%	3025910	53%	2653189	47%
3.	Chhattisgarh	20833803	1532465	7.4%	705427	46%	827038	54%
4.	Jharkhand	26945829	1611970	6.0%	808122	50%	803848	50%
5.	Madhya Pradesh	60348023	4440447	7.4%	2177905	49%	2262542	51%
6.	Orissa	36804660	3101162	8.4%	1537109	50%	1564053	50%
7.	Sikkim	540851	30978	5.7%	17433	56%	13545	44%
8.	Uttar Pradesh	166197921	12386379	7.5%	6582650	53%	5803729	47%
	India	**1028610328**	**79360793**	**7.7%**	**39268889**	**49%**	**40091904**	**51%**

Source: Handbook on Social Welfare Statistics, 2004, Ministry of Social Justice and Empowerment, Govt. of India, New Delhi.

20.1 per cent of urban population, but it also has a substantial component of tribal population. Its literacy rate is 65.18 per cent, which includes 77.86 per cent of male and 52.4 per cent of female. Work participation rate in Chhattisgarh is 46.54 per cent. In the case of females, it is 40.04 per cent while among males it is 52.97 per cent. Handbook on Social Statistics, 2004, Ministry of Social Justice and Empowerment shows that 37.87 per cent of people in Chhattisgarh live below poverty line.

Jharkhand: It is also a newly created state. It has a population of nearly 2269 lakhs. In the state, 22.2 per cent of the population lives in urban areas. Literacy rate is 54.13 per cent (male: 67.94 per cent; female: 39.38 per cent). Turning to work participation rate, the state has quite low proportion of people working as main or marginal workers.

Rate of work participation is merely 37.64 per cent, with 48.21 per cent among males and 26.4 per cent among females. As per recent official statistics available with Ministry of Social Justice and Empowerment, 42.6 per cent population in the state (same as Bihar) lives below the poverty line.

Madhya Pradesh: It stands as the seventh largest state according to population size. In the state, 26.7 per cent population lives in urban areas. Literacy rate, in consonance with the national average, is 64.11 per cent, with 76.8 per cent male and 50.28 per cent female. Further, work participation rate is 42.75 per cent that comprises 51.62 per cent males and 33.1 per cent females. The proportion of persons living below the poverty line in the state is 37.87 per cent. The state is at the twelfth place on Human Development Index.

Orissa: According to Census 2001, Orissa has nearly 368 lakh population. Among its 30 districts, Ganjam is not only the most populous one, but also a source of maximum out-migration. The state has a total urban population of 15 per cent, almost a half of the national average. Literacy rate in Orissa is a shade better than other states. It is 63.61 per cent (males: 75.95 per cent; females: 50.97 per cent). Work participation rate is low, the rich natural resources of the state notwithstanding. Among males, work participation rate is 52.75 per cent while among females it is 24.62 per cent, with the state average of 38.88 per cent. Economic conditions are rather discouraging, 47.15 per cent of population lives below the poverty line. Further, the state ranks eleventh on Human Development Index.

Sikkim: One of the north-eastern states, Sikkim has a population of about 5 lakhs only. Only 11.1 per cent of the population in the state is urban. It has a literacy rate of about 70 per cent — 76.7 per cent males and 61.46 per cent females are literate. However, work participation rate in the state is only 48.72 per cent (males: 57.58 per cent; females 38.59 per cent). In Sikkim, 36.55 per cent population lives below poverty line.

Uttar Pradesh: According to the census of 2001, the population of the state is nearly 1661 lakhs. Literacy rate is 57.3 per cent, with 70.23 per cent males and 42.98 per cent females. Work participation rate in Uttar Pradesh is 32.6 per cent (47.26 per cent males and 16.28 per cent females). The urban population component in the state is 20.8 per cent. In the state, 31.15 per cent population is estimated to live below the poverty line. On Human Development Index, Uttar Pradesh figures at the thirteenth place.

The Table 3.3 presents district wise number and proportion of elderly under the study states.

Personal Background

Having discussed generally the social context, we need to take a close look or provide a micro-level analysis. Given this, attention may now be paid to such personal characteristics as age, marital status, educational background, occupational status, and type of family of the respondents in the study.

Age Distribution: Increasing age apparently brings greater dependence on others making the elderly somewhat vulnerable. Though at varying levels, advancing age brings in deteriorative ailments coupled with decreasing sensory capacities. Considering the factor of age, family, community and society distribute resources and allocate roles. It may be noted that within 'old age' there are various subgroups based on age, and these subgroups have differential needs and problems.

In the study, the age of the elderly women ranges from 60 to 103 years. Value of mode as well as of median is 65 years,

Table 3.3: Population of Aged Persons (60 and above) in Sampled Districts

Sl. No.	*Name of State*	*Total Population (All Ages)*	*Total Aged Population*		*Sex-wise Population of Aged*			
					Male		*Female*	
			No.	*Per cent*	*No.*	*Per cent*	*No.*	*Per cent*
1.	**Assam**	**26655528**	**1589340**	**6.0**	**817793**	**51**	**771547**	**49**
	Goalpara	822035	45302	5.5	21603	48	23699	52
	Sonitpur	1681513	95220	5.7	50794	53	44426	47
	Tinsukia	1252019	70346	5.6	38102	54	32244	46
	Kachar	1444921	98249	6.8	50411	51	47838	49
2.	**Bihar**	**82998509**	**5679099**	**6.8**	**3025910**	**53**	**2653189**	**47**
	Madhubani	35725281	241753	0.7	123594	51	118159	49
	Kathihar	2583511	144870	5.6	74976	52	69894	48
	Nawada	1809696	125403	6.9	66913	53	58490	47
	Saran	3248701	262668	8.1	137401	52	125267	48
3.	**Chhattisgarh**	**20833803**	**1532465**	**7.4**	**705427**	**46**	**827038**	**54**
	Koria	586327	35690	6.1	17358	49	18332	51
	Raigarh	1381437	114904	8.3	52900	46	62004	54
	Dhamtari	706591	53756	7.6	23734	44	30022	56

Sl. No.	Name of State	Total Population (All Ages)	Total Aged Population		Sex-wise Population of Aged			
					Male		Female	
			No.	Per cent	No.	Per cent	No.	Per cent
	Kabirdham	584552	42930	7.3	19554	46	23376	54
4.	**Jharkhand**	**26945829**	**1611970**	**6.0**	**808122**	**50**	**803848**	**50**
	Garhwa	1035464	68843	6.6	36835	54	32008	46
	Hazaribag	2404744	135372	5.6	67672	50	67700	50
	Dumka	1759602	105001	6.0	49956	48	55045	52
	West Singhbhum	2082795	121244	5.8	55417	46	65827	54
5.	**Madhya Pradesh**	**60348023**	**4440447**	**7.4**	**2177905**	**49**	**2262542**	**51**
	Gwalior	2459135	162109	6.6	79988	49	82121	51
	Umaria	515963	34654	6.7	17274	50	17380	50
	Indore	3970889	282641	7.1	138174	49	144467	51
	Betul	1395175	108112	7.7	52637	49	55475	51
6.	**Orissa**	**36804660**	**3101162**	**8.4**	**1537109**	**50**	**1564053**	**50**
	Sundargarh	1830673	127003	6.9	63177	50	63826	50
	Cuttack	2875748	270393	9.4	139014	51	131379	49

Sl. No.	Name of State	Total Population (All Ages)	Total Aged Population		Sex-wise Population of Aged			
					Male		Female	
			No.	Per cent	No.	Per cent	No.	Per cent
	Ganjjam	3160635	279330	8.8	138202	49	141128	51
	Bolangir	1337194	127724	9.6	60488	47	67236	53
7.	**Sikkim**	**540851**	**30978**	**5.7**	**17433**	**56**	**13545**	**44**
	North District	41030	2539	6.2	1468	58	1071	42
	West District	123256	7562	6.1	4205	56	3357	44
	South District	131525	7786	5.9	4373	56	3413	44
	East District	245040	13091	5.3	7387	56	5704	44
8.	**Uttar Pradesh**	**166197921**	**12386379**	**7.5**	**6582650**	**53**	**5803729**	**47**
	Aligarh	3661373	255202	7.0	131991	52	123211	48
	Barielly	4338904	253910	5.9	132441	52	121469	48
	Jhansi	2171129	164765	7.6	83074	50	81691	50
	Gorakhpur	4392157	333989	7.6	178804	54	155185	46
	India	**1028610328**	**79360793**	**7.7**	**39268889**	**49**	**40091904**	**51**

Source: Census of India 2001.

and mean is 67 years of elderly women. The mean age of their husbands (70 years) is slightly higher than elderly women. In order to facilitate further analysis, three age categories have been developed. These include 37 per cent respondents in the age-group of 60 to 64 years, named as 'young elderly', 49 per cent in 65 to 74 years category, termed as 'old elderly' and 14 per cent in 75 to 99 years, named as 'old-old elderly'.

It is assumed that the needs and problems, adjustment to age related changes are different in young, old and old-old age groups. Old-old age groups are considered frail and dependent while the elderly in younger age groups are more autonomous and productive. Let us take a look at state-wise distribution of respondents in various age groups (Table 3.4).

Table 3.4: State-wise distribution of age of respondents and their husband (Percentage)

State	*Elderly women*			*Husband*		
	Young	*Old*	*Old-old*	*Young*	*Old*	*Old-old*
Assam	44	46	10	6	76	18
Bihar	37	48	16	7	75	18
Chhattisgarh	27	62	11	7	74	19
Jharkhand	42	43	15	6	73	21
Madhya Pradesh	36	50	14	7	76	19
Orissa	36	47	17	4	64	32
Sikkim	46	42	12	15	66	17
Uttar Pradesh	31	52	17	4	71	25
Total	**37**	**49**	**14**	**8**	**71**	**21**

Data show that while age of husband of old women is more skewed towards 'old' age group, that is, 65 to 74 years, elderly women are more often in young and old categories. Sikkim may be taken as the 'youngest' state while Orissa and Uttar Pradesh as 'oldest'.

Ageing often leads to health problems and dependence on others in activities of daily living. This is what is exemplified by the situation of Bhagirati. Among other things, Case Study (3.01) brings out how ageing adds to the vulnerability among elderly women.

Case History 3.1
Long Life: Bliss or Curse?

Bhagirati is 79-year-old elderly woman living in a village of Bareilly. She has stooping gait and wrinkled face and haggard looks. Her body has become a hub of ailments. She is suffering from urinary incontinency and high blood pressure. As she is a diabetic, her cataract operation is also being postponed.

Bhagirati is dependent on others for getting up and sitting. Her medicine and treatment costs are increasing steadily. The daughter-in-law and grandchildren find it difficult to provide care and attention to the frail ageing lady. Though Bhagirati doesn't have obvious financial constraints, increasing health problems are making her suffer in many ways. Her interaction with neighbours and relatives has decreased.

Religious Affiliations: According to Wolff (1959) religious beliefs, prayer and faith in god, all help the aged to overcome problems like loneliness, grief and unhappiness. Added to this, it is assumed that elderly play a very important role in guiding and performing religious rites. It helps in their integration in the family and community.

In India, Hindus form the largest religious group followed by Muslims, Sikhs and Christians. In the study, 85 per cent respondents are Hindu, 9 per cent Muslims, 1 per cent Christians and 0.2 per cent Sikhs. Table 3.5 provides comparative view of religion-wise distribution of respondents.

Table 3.5: Respondents by Religion (Percentages)

State	*Christian*	*Hindu*	*Muslim*	*Others*	*Total*
Assam	—	80	19	1	100
Bihar	—	81	18	1	100
Chhattisgarh	—	95	5	—	100
Jharkhand	1	89	9	1	100
Madhya Pradesh	1	90	7	2	100
Orissa	3	95	1	1	100
Sikkim	4	66	1	29	100
Uttar Pradesh	—	82	18	—	100
Total	1	**85**	**10**	**4**	**100**

It is seen that Orissa followed by Chhattisgarh and Madhya Pradesh has a predominantly Hindu population, more than 90 per cent. Assam, Uttar Pradesh and Bihar have substantially high proportion of Muslim population when seen in the context of national trends. Sikkim has almost one-third of the population professing other religions like Buddhism.

Quite interestingly, district level analysis shows that in Assam, Goalpara (35 per cent) and Kachar (30 per cent) have almost one-third elderly respondents professing Islam.

In Uttar Pradesh, Aligarh (24 per cent) and Bareilly (33 per cent) have Muslim domination while Gorakhpur (94 per cent) and Jhansi (93 per cent) have majority of Hindu population. All the four districts of Chhattisgarh – Koriya (94 per cent), Raigarh (96 per cent), Dhamtri (94 per cent) and Kabirdham (95 per cent) are Hindu dominated. North district of Sikkim has 56 per cent respondents belonging to other religions like Buddhism.

Caste: Caste-system is a unique characteristic of Hindu society. This age-old institution has stratified the society into four *varnas* — Brahmin, Kashtriya, Vaishya and Shudra. As in the present form, it is rigidly hereditary.

The caste-system imposes certain restrictions on its

members in the matter of occupation as well as social intercourse. After Independence, Government of India has tried to improve the situation of the underprivileged sections, officially termed as — Scheduled Castes (SC), Scheduled Tribes (ST) and Other Backward Classes (OBC) — through several affirmative actions. During last 50 years, among other changes, in caste norms, occupation has tended to become independent of caste affiliation. Let us see the situation in the present study.

Table 3.6: Respondents by Caste (Percentages)

States	*SC*	*ST*	*BC/OBC*	*Others*	*Total*
Assam	23	6	38	34	100
Bihar	17	12	52	18	100
Chhattisgarh	24	28	46	2	100
Jharkhand	21	17	50	12	100
Madhya Pradesh	30	17	42	12	100
Orissa	24	19	50	7	100
Sikkim	4	42	48	6	100
Uttar Pradesh	24	6	49	21	100
Total	21	18	47	14	100

In the present study sample, 21 per cent elderly women are in the category of Scheduled Caste, 18 per cent in Scheduled Tribes, and 47 per cent in backward class/other backward class. Only 14 per cent of them belong to other caste groups, presumably Brahmin, Kshatriya, Vaishya, etc.

Table 3.6 gives the state-wise distribution of caste. Madhya Pradesh has maximum proportion of respondents belonging to Scheduled Caste, followed by Uttar Pradesh and Chhattisgarh. In the case of Scheduled Tribe respondents, Sikkim dominates the list. Bihar has maximum proportion of respondents belonging to BC/OBC category, followed by Jharkhand and Orissa. Does caste influence vulnerability among elderly women? This dimension will be analysed a little later.

Marital Status: It plays a crucial role in identity formation, social, emotional and economic well-being, especially in the case of women. Patriarchal social structure has always expected women to be dependent on her husband in her youth. A high value is attached to the marital status of woman, and widowhood, separation, divorce are taken as 'curse' on her.

For example, widowhood not only brings bereavement but also an associated loss of status, discrimination, loss of economic power and lowering of self-esteem. In addition, widowhood is often accompanied by tacit handicaps and even restrictions in her domestic and social spheres. In certain cultural groups, a widow is considered inauspicious in social and religious activities. As a result, she is given a differential and unequal treatment. She is treated as an object of collective discrimination (Jamuna, 1995). In the Indian social context, widowhood seems to enhance vulnerability.

In the study, 38 per cent respondents are married, 60 per cent widow, one per cent divorced/separated and one per cent unmarried. It may be noted that since the proportion of unmarried, separated and divorced aged women in the study is very small, these categories have been merged with that of widow. Results show a consistency in the proportion of married and widow respondents in rural as well as urban areas. In rural areas, there are 39 per cent married and 62 per cent widows while in urban areas corresponding figures of married and widow respondents are 37 per cent and 63 per cent respectively.

State-wise analysis of marital status of respondents brings out that the highest proportion of widows is in Assam (71 per cent) followed by Uttar Pradesh (66 per cent), Madhya Pradesh and Jharkhand (64 per cent each). Highest proportion of married respondents are in Sikkim (55 per cent), followed by Orissa (41 per cent), Bihar (39 per cent) and Chhattisgarh (38 per cent). The situation of widow elderly could be taken to be at risk of helplessness or in the situation of vulnerability.

Let us look at the relation, if any, between the marital status of the elderly women and their age. Findings show that the proportion of elderly widows is almost double the proportion of married elderly women. Analysis further brings out that in the age-group of 60 to 64 years, 49 per cent respondents are widowed. The corresponding proportion, in the category of 65 to 74 years, is 65 per cent. In the age-group of 75 to 103 years,

84 per cent respondents are widows. Statistical analysis shows that rank correlation between marital status and age of the respondents is sizable (rank correlation = 0.24). Diagram 3.1 gives the marital status of elderly women in the study.

Diagram 3.1

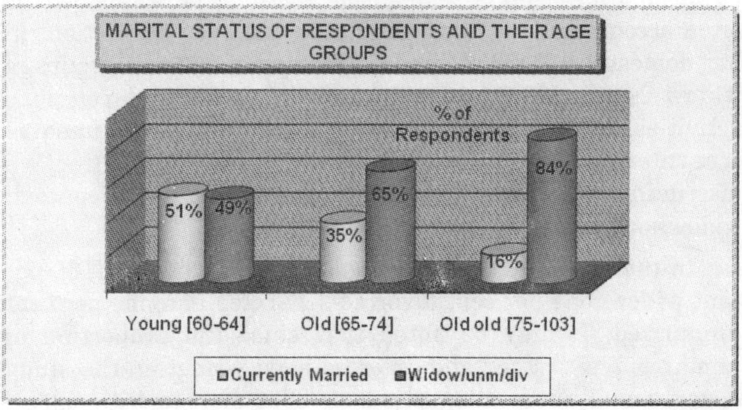

Qualitative data delineated below show that vulnerability among elderly women increases when their husband is not in the scene. Case studies of Saraswati and Musmi Devi given below portray the amount of vulnerability they are exposed to:

Case History 3.2

Widowhood: A curse?

Saraswati is 62 years. She lives in a village in Aligarh. Her three sons and two daughters are married and settled in life. Her daughters-in-law are housewife. After widowhood, her status changed drastically. Daughters-in-law have started shouting at her on tiny issues. Her routine needs like nutrition, health, and the like were denied in a subtle manner.

At present, Saraswati has persistent health problems like cough and digestive upsets. Now she lives away from her natural family in a *jhompri* in the same village. Indeed, she needs help in activities of daily living and also for medical care. But is there anyone to stand by her?

Case History 3.3

Desertion: What is my mistake?

Musmi Devi is a 60-year old (deserted) lady. A couple of months after her marriage, her husband left her for good. She was sent back to her parents' house. And now four decades down the line, her parents are no more on the scene. Long back, her brother migrated with family to a city. She is now alone in the household. In-laws never looked back. She was blamed for not being able to hold back her husband throughout her life. No efforts were ever made to remarry her off. In the neighbourhood, Musmi's niece stays who provides her food and helps in meeting her daily needs. To raise some extra money, she also works as maid in the neighbourhood, that is, whenever her health permits.

In contrast, there are elderly people who plan, howsoever loosely, for their old age. Further-more, they are in control of their finances and their affairs — and lead relatively a peaceful and contended old age. This is what is illustrated by the lifestyle of Sharda:

Case History 3.4

Zenith of old age

Sharda Devi, 64, is a retired teacher living in a village of Aligarh. She lives in a joint family with sons, daughters-in-law and grandchildren. Her husband is a retired clerk. Together, they get a pension of Rs. 5000 a month. She contributes Rs. 4000 for their upkeep to the family. In fact, Sharda and her husband have few financial worries. Worth of rupees fifteen lakhs, the house is in her name. She has a room exclusively for herself and husband.

Sharda is consulted for every big and small decision in the family. She has good relations with all her family members, and even with distant relatives. She leads a peaceful and contented life, often dreamt of by most old women.

These case studies also show that marital status is quite significant in influencing self-concept and social-acceptance of elderly women. Often times, women lose status in the family and community once they are widow. Does widowhood add to social vulnerability of elderly women?

Educational Level: It is often held that education leads to empowerment. Education is believed to inculcate knowledge, understanding, confidence and independence. It follows that, generally speaking, illiterate people would tend to be more vulnerable than literate or educated ones. Kumar (1991) observes that educational attainment has a bearing on the financial condition as well as living standards. Unfortunately, educational status of the elderly, in our country, presents a discouraging picture. In 2001, literacy among elderly males was merely 27 per cent, and that among aged females it was all the more disheartening — just 13 per cent. It was far below the national average of 52.2 per cent. Let us examine (Table 3.7) the educational status of the elderly women under study.

In this study, most of the elderly women (93 per cent) are illiterate. Only seven per cent elderly women are literate. Within the literate category, five per cent have never gone to school. Another 69 per cent of them have studied up to primary class, 19 per cent up to middle, five per cent up to tenth and just two per cent have been to college. Only four respondents (0.1 per cent) have done post-graduation. Mean years of schooling compute to 1.17. It is evident that literacy and education have not been very popular or prevalent among women and girls, particularly in the preceding century. Given this, educational status of elderly women has been divided for further analysis into two categories – illiterate and literate/educated. Table 3.7 also provides state-wise distribution of educational status of elderly women.

This apart, data analysis brings out that only 30 per cent husbands of the respondents are literate as compared with seven per cent of women. Out of them, one per cent elderly males (husband) are literate but had no schooling, 12 per cent have studied up to primary, seven per cent up to middle-school and five per cent have passed tenth standard. Merely six per cent elderly males have studied up to twelfth and above. Males

Table 3.7: Educational Level of the Elderly Women

State	*Illiterate*	*Percent out of Literate / Educated*					
		Literate, no schooling	*Up to Primary*	*Up to Middle*	*Up to 10th*	*Up to 12th & +*	*Total*
Assam	79	1	74	21	5	0	100
Bihar	98	0	79	16	5	0	100
Chhattisgarh	97	3	83	10	0	3	100
Jharkhand	94	7	55	29	5	4	100
Madhya Pradesh	96	11	64	11	6	8	100
Orissa	89	9	75	8	6	2	100
Sikkim	92	3	63	24	9	1	100
Uttar Pradesh	96	18	45	26	5	5	100

are certainly better off in terms of literacy and education than their female counterparts, but only marginally so.

Diagram 3.2

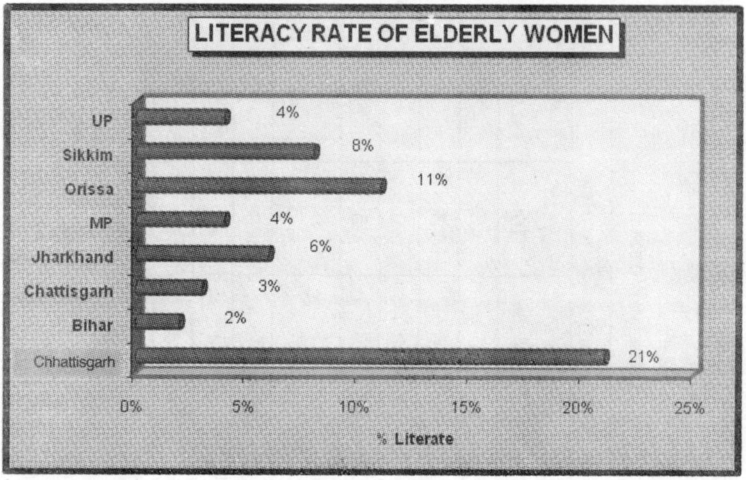

Diagram 3.2 depicts literacy rate of elderly women in the study states. Literacy rate is generally low among elderly women. Assam has most elderly women in the category of literate/educated. Bihar followed by Chhattisgarh, Madhya Pradesh and Uttar Pradesh has maximum number of illiterate elderly women. Lower literacy rate among females in the state is in consonance with that of the elderly women. Quite interestingly, Orissa presents a brighter picture, especially when the state is one of the most economically backward states in the country.

Apparently, low educational status among the elderly may be due to lack of opportunities for the elderly who were born around the time of Independence or before it. Literacy rate is likely to be better among the young elderly as compared to old-old ones. The unduly large rate of illiteracy could also be attributed to indifferent schooling facilities during their childhood as well as cultural constraints in the way of female education.

Family Background: Not only does family, as a social institution, meets basic needs of its members, whether they are children, adults or elderly, but also it provides them love, care, and security. Often, the latter is taken as a very important safeguard against vulnerability. Dandekar (1996) notes that old men and women in India prefer to live with their (grownup) children more often than those in Western countries.

In part, this may explain as to why welfare institutions for the aged such as residential homes, in India, are not very popular. Given these considerations, attention needs to be focused on family-related aspects.

Area: Place of living as well as socio-cultural milieu influence the well-being of the aged. Likewise, rural-urban characteristics also have a bearing on their psyche. Needless to add, urban family groups markedly differ from rural family groups. These differences are noticeable in terms of structure, size, mode of production and consumption, interpersonal relations, etc. Equally important is the consideration of impersonality, almost inherent in urban environment, in contrast to cohesion and bonding in rural community (Khan and Kaushik, 1999).

In the study, sample-design specified one-third of the respondents from urban areas and two-thirds from rural ones. Below are some of the qualitative data in the form of case studies that reflect the differential experiences of destitute elderly women in rural and urban contexts.

The case of Zohra Khatun underlines the situation of destitute elderly women in urban areas.

Case History 3.5

Unfavourable Urban Environment

Zohra Khatun is a 60 years old Muslim widow who lives in Hazaribagh, all alone as she has no children or close relatives. She is illiterate. She has no source of income. By way of property, she owns a small kutcha (mud) house that provides only partial protection during rainy or cold season. Her health is indifferent. She often complaints of coughs, breathing troubles and digestive upsets. She intends to visit a doctor but has been postponing the visit.

To keep body and soul together, Zohra begs in a nearby locality, and whatever little she gets, she tries to maintain herself within that. Even then, many nights she sleeps with empty stomach. She fulfils necessary conditions for social assistance — pension or food grain. She has also tried for these; but luck is yet to smile at her.

In contrast, the situation of the elderly in rural area is a shade better. Let us examine the case of Kaushik Bai;

Case History 3.6

Supportive Village

Kaushik Bai, 70, is a widow who lives in a small village in Betul (MP). Thin and frail, she cannot walk without the support of a walking stick. She lives in a kutcha house. Her son stays in a nearby brick house but she is not allowed entry there. Earlier, she was granted Old Age Pension but it was stopped three years ago, as her close relatives, including her son, are around. She has repeatedly approached the village *sarpancha* to restart her pension but nothing happened. In the meanwhile, community people are looking after her and providing her food and shelter.

Case History 3.7

Solace in Joint Family

Vishnobai is a 70-year old married woman, living in a village, some distance away from Gwalior. Her house is rather big. Built on a 500 sqft. plot, it has nine rooms. And why not? Her five married sons, their wives, and grandchildren live in the big house. Her sons earn and pool their income to be appropriated by their parents. She is in the centre of family affairs, and virtually all decisions are made by her. A year back, she developed stones; and she got herself operated in a private hospital.

Vishnobai is quite satisfied with her life, and lives gracefully with her married sons and grandchildren. Her family members and her large household keep her pleasantly busy.

The case studies bring out the difference of locale. Urban areas tend to accentuate vulnerability, destitution and sufferings while in rural areas, whatever meager social support can be expected.

Family Background

Like others, the elderly also need the support and security of the family. Family-type determines, to some extent, the kind of support and carc the elderly can get. In this regard, security and well-being of the aged, to a large extent, have been ensured by joint family groups (Gangrade, 1989). On the other hand, nuclear family groups, though becoming the trend of the day, are too person-centred to favour the situation of the elderly (Khan, 1997).

In the present study, 41 per cent respondents are from nuclear family groups, that is, with their unmarried children and/or husband. Nonetheless, majority of the elderly (59 per cent) have been living in joint/extended families. Diagram 3.3 represents the type of family of the respondents. Unlike the popular belief that nuclear families are more common in urban areas and joint families are a norm in rural areas, data show that there is no difference in the proportion of type of family and the location.

Diagram 3.3

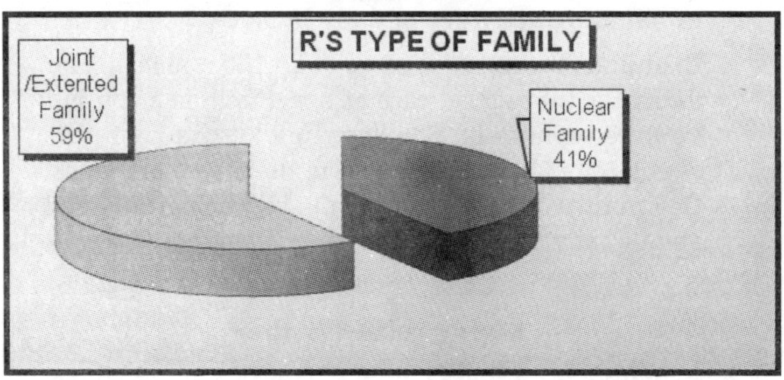

However, every elderly woman cannot be as lucky as Vishnobai. To many others, not having the conducive support of family, only dream of a contended life and, for them, old age becomes yet another struggle for existence.

Data further show that 96 per cent of the elderly women are staying in natural family, and four per cent in some other family, say, with their married daughter, sister, brother-in-law, friends, etc. Apparently, not being able to stay in natural family often aggravates the vulnerable condition of elderly women. Among those not staying in the natural family, 45 per cent are staying with parents/married brother/sister, another 42 per cent are staying with married daughters, six per cent are with nephew/niece and another six per cent are with friends/neighbours. The main reasons for not staying with the natural family are — only son/all sons migrated, thrown out of family, rude behaviour of daughter-in-law, etc. Below are typical case studies of a few elderly women who are not with their natural family:

Case History 3.8

Staying with Married Daughter

Bismillat is 103 years old. She is a widow. She lives with her daughter's family who too is 60 years of age. Illiterate with craggy skin, grey hair, bowed gait, a false denture, financially she is not unsound. Added to this, her health is poor. She requires help in handling activities of daily living.

Bismillat receives a pension of Rs.150 a month. Her daughter takes good care of her. She has a son but he lives separately. She lives in a kutcha house. As she is too old, she is unable to do household work. Community people prop her up, psychologically and emotionally.

Case History 3.9

Living with Brother

Arakhiya is 99 years old. She lives in a small village in Dumka, Jharkhand, with her brother. She has never been to school. She does not do any work, only wander in the village the whole day, and chat with neighbours. Her husband died early in age.

> But her brother and his family take good care of her.

Arakhia often complains about joint pain. She has lost her vision partially. Family members and others in the community give her due respect. Her economic condition is all right. She keeps herself fresh and tidy. She is satisfied with her life.

Case History 3.10

Living alone Hurts

> Chanmoni Begam, 65, appears weak and older than her age. She lives alone in a hut and all the time thinks about her son who left her in the evening of her life. She desperately needs him. Her two daughters are married and well settled in their life. She works as a maid and earns Rs. 300 per month. Her husband passed away 12 years ago. Her eyesight is weak and she is unable to do much work.
>
> Chanmoni is not getting any social assistance from the state, though she is a genuine indigent person. She wants to get admission in an Old Age Home because she feels insecure in living alone.

Size of the Household

No denying the fact that in large sized households elderly people have a higher level of comfort. On the other hand, the present study shows that 10.5 per cent of elderly are living alone, which largely conforms to the national average of 11.1 per cent (Census 2001). 'Living alone' of elderly women escalates their vulnerability manifolds. It signifies social, emotional, economic vulnerability. They are easy target for crime victimisation. When sick or lonely, they hardly have anyone to provide support. In a nutshell, elderly women living alone would attract a clear vulnerability.

Data further bring out that 33 per cent of elderly respondents have small family size comprising 2 to 4 members, 27 per cent have medium (5 to 6 members) and 27 per cent have large (7 to 24 members) family size. Mean size of family is found to be 5.04 (median is 5, and mode is 6 members). Data are heterogeneous (SD = 2.9). Result also reflects that location is not associated with size of family. There is consistency in the proportion of family size of respondents in rural and urban areas.

In this connection, an assessment of the number of children of the respondents would be insightful. Children, particularly sons, are considered as some sort of a security in old age. In the present study, 45 per cent respondents have a few children (1 to 2), 55 per cent have several (3 to 10) children and the rest remained quiet on this issue. Coming to number of married or unmarried sons, 41 per cent have one son, 59 per cent have several (2 to 9) sons and rest of them have not furnished any information in this regard. Further, 48 per cent elderly women have one married daughter and 52 per cent have several (2 to 10) married daughters. Rest of the respondents either do not have daughters or did not mention anything about them. Location wise comparison of children of elderly women brings out no significant variation between rural and urban locations.

Exposure to Media

In this technologically fast world, newspapers, television, radio and other media of mass communication have provided easy and rapid access to information. They are the vibrant tools of information, education and entertainment.

Study results however show that most of the respondents (83 per cent) are not inclined to use mass media channels. Only 29 per cent listen to radio, 69 per cent watch television, one per cent read newspapers, magazines, and one per cent elderly women make use of all the mentioned media channels for infotainment purposes.

Table 3.8 gives the details of respondents' exposure to media in various study states. It shows that elderly women in Bihar, Chhattisgarh, Madhya Pradesh, Uttar Pradesh often do not make use of media like radio, television, newspapers, etc. Listening radio is more popular in Assam and Sikkim. Newspapers and magazines do not attract the attention of most of elderly respondents irrespective of states.

Table 3.8: Exposure to Media (Percentage)

State	*No Exposure*	*Per cent of Those Who have Exposure to Media*				
		Listen Radio	*Watch T.V.*	*Newspaper*	*Most of them*	*Any Other*
Assam	90	41	58	1	—	1
Bihar	95	25	75	—	—	—
Chhattisgarh	94	46	54	—	—	—
Jharkhand	88	20	80	—	1	—
Madhya Pradesh	93	22	73	—	2	3
Orissa	83	27	70	—	1	2
Sikkim	49	23	75	1	—	1
Uttar Pradesh	90	29	61	3	4	3
Total	**83**	**29**	**69**	**1**	**1**	**1**

It is often held that elderly women face triple jeopardy — on account of being elderly, being women, and being economically dependent. In this section, various socio-demographic factors of elderly have been looked into. Qualitative data expressed vulnerability because of age, living in urban milieu and other than natural families. Widowhood, type and size of family are significant variables that influence vulnerability of elderly women. These and other factors accentuating or curbing vulnerability among elderly women would be discussed at length in subsequent sections.

4

Livelihood Issues

Economic independence is considered as one of the most important components of well-being of the elderly. This theme has been a central concern of international fora and the United Nations, and it has been duly emphasised in India in the National Policy on Older Persons.

Often old age tends to bring in its wake economic dependence. In fact, retirement from the work-life is generally considered as the beginning point of old age, especially among men. In the case of elderly women, situation is quite different. Patriarchal social structure has seldom realised women's economic worth. Economic value of women invariably remains invisible. It is neither remunerated nor acknowledged. Their productive role in the domestic responsibilities mostly goes unnoticed, unaccounted for and un-remunerated. In spite of their being economically active, they generally remain economically dependent on their family. Besides, there are reinforcing circumstances. As a majority of elderly women does not participate in paid work outside home, their economic independence is hardly an issue. Given this, economic insecurity and vulnerability are obvious consequences.

Were there factors that ensured security of the aged in yester-years? Agrarian economy encouraged and supported joint family system. So, staying together of three to four generations under one roof was the common practice. In the joint family system, property ownership would be in the hands of *karta*, the eldest male in the family. He would control the family's property, income and expenditure. Among others, it ensured security and authority to the aged. Often, the status and security of an elderly woman would be directly related to her husband's position in the family. Should she be wife of the head of the family, she would have to herself an important niche in the family that ensured her security and status. Correspondingly, other elderly women, too, would have status in the family and would be looked after properly (see Panda, 2005).

However, the present-day conditions are markedly different. Industrialisation has, by and large, changed the earning patterns of the people. In many rural areas, fragmentation of land-holdings over generations has made agriculture economically unviable. Unemployment and underemployment in rural areas is one of the major 'push factors' — escalating village-to-city movement. On the other hand, migration affects elderly women the most. Grown-up sons, who are often taken as 'security' in old age, take to industrial centres or cities in search of economic opportunities. Often they take their wife and children along, leaving the aged, including their mother, behind to fend for themselves.

Urban areas are characterised by intense competition in almost all walks of life. Job market favours the young who have educational background or technical skills. On the other hand, knowledge and skills of the elderly are, more often than not, taken as outdated. The headship of the family has also changed, from the oldest to the bread earner, usually far younger in age. All these factors appear to combine to slowly undermine the traditional and ascribed status of the aged. They are fast emerging as a vulnerable group. Prominent in this are aged females who have almost always been economically dependent.

Typically, a woman in India successively identifies herself with her father, husband and subsequently with son. In her old age, she is socially and economically dependent either on her husband or (mostly) son. This is what makes an elderly woman much more vulnerable than her male counterpart. Prakash (1996) raises a pertinent question, "If men, who were once active in the labour force, are considered as 'burden',

Table 4.1: Distribution of Aged persons by Status of Economic Independence in Sex and residence in India in 1995-96 (Percentage)

Dependency	*Rural*			*Urban*		
	Male	*Female*	*Total*	*Male*	*Female*	*Total*
Independent	49	12	30	52	12	31
Partially Dependent	18	15	16	17	11	14
Fully Dependent	31	71	51	30	76	53
Persons supporting partially/fully dependent elderly						
Spouse	11	16	14	11	18	16
Offspring	77	72	74	79	70	73
Grandchildren	5	5	5	5	6	6
Others	7	7	7	5	7	6

Source: NSSO, 52nd Round.

then what about women who always had been invisible contributors?" Does it influence the security of the elderly women?

The foregoing discussion brings out that age tends to increase economic dependence in the elderly, particularly in elderly women. In turn, this engenders and enhances vulnerability. Women, who have been dependent on others almost throughout their life, often become more susceptible to vulnerability. Table 4.1 provides estimates of economic dependence-independence of elderly persons in rural and urban areas.

Table 4.1 abundantly shows that women are more dependent on others than their male counterparts. Also, urban elderly women are more dependent than the rural ones. Further, more than 71 per cent of elderly women are fully dependent on 'significant others'. Likewise, it is observed that most of the elderly are dependent on their offspring. This, in part, explains as to why sons are considered to be security in old age. To what an extent is economic dependence related to vulnerability?

Occupational Status

Often occupational status provides an indication of the economic position, self-confidence and life-style of a person. Those working in the government or public sector undertaking, have to retire at or around the age of 60 years. Conversely, for those working in unorganised sectors, their time of superannuation is largely determined by their physical and mental health conditions. Jobs like labour work, harvesting, hand-embroidery, etc. require physical strength as also sound sensory capabilities. As such, younger persons usually replace the elderly who face a waning of their prowess. In this respect, what is the situation of the elderly women?

Before proceeding further, let us examine the occupational pattern of elderly women (Table 4.2).

Table 4.2: State-wise Distribution of Occupational Pattern of Elderly Women (Percentage)

State	*Non-Workers/ Housewife*	*Classification of Occupations*				
		Daily Wager	*Agri-culture*	*Business*	*Salaried Job*	*Pension*
Assam	56	16	7	8	17	51
Bihar	57	41	7	10	4	39
Chhattisgarh	61	77	6	9	3	6
Jharkhand	56	27	28	11	8	26
Madhya Pradesh	57	43	9	12	7	28
Orissa	53	42	8	11	6	32
Sikkim	51	11	26	8	2	52
Uttar Pradesh	71	49	20	13	4	13
Total	**58**	**37**	**14**	**10**	**7**	**32**

Source: NSSO, 52nd Round.

In the present study, more than a half (58 per cent) of the respondents have been housewife or non-workers. Among workers, 37 per cent have been daily wagers and 14 per cent agriculture workers. Another ten per cent are into business and three per cent are into salaried job. There are 32 per cent elderly women getting pension.

Table 4.2 brings out that highest proportion of non-workers is in Uttar Pradesh and lowest proportion is in Sikkim. While Chhattisgarh has the largest number of daily wagers, Sikkim has the smallest. Further, Sikkim and Jharkhand have more elderly women earning their livelihood as agricultural workers. Uttar Pradesh has the highest proportion of elderly women into business, and Assam and Sikkim have the lowest. In Sikkim, almost one-fourth of the elderly women are getting pension; in contrast, this proportion is lowest in Chhattisgarh. Do the states also differ in terms of economic vulnerability?

Turning attention to the present occupation of the husband of elderly women, it is found that eight per cent are daily-wage earners, seven per cent agricultural workers, four per cent businessmen, three per cent pensioners and just one per cent salaried workers.

Data on occupational status show that there are more or less similar proportions of elderly men and women in various categories of occupation with one notable exception. In the category of wage earners, proportion of the elderly women is almost double their male counterparts. This suggests that elderly women have to resort to hard physical labour to raise a living, and that they are more vulnerable. Below is the case study of a lady who, in her old age, has to take up vegetable-vending to sustain herself.

Case History 4.1

Sustaining livelihood in old age

> Nazbun, 70 years, has been a housewife all her life. She has never got the opportunity or even felt the need to take up work or job. Her husband was earning enough to feed the family. However, they were not able to save money for old age, nor had they any property or assets. Somehow, they could manage to get their three daughters married off.

> After the demise of husband, Nazbun felt vulnerable — economically, socially and emotionally. She was all alone with hardly any means of livelihood. All she could think of was to take to selling vegetables and to earn some money to make both ends meet.
>
> As vegetable vendor, Nazbun earns 20 to 30 rupees a day. She lives in a rented accommodation for which she pays 200 rupees a month. She wants to open a general-store, but does not have enough resources.

Table 4.3 presents a comparative view of the occupation pursued by the elderly women and their husband in rural and urban setting. It shows that in the category of non-workers, proportion of women is more than their male counterparts, both in rural and urban areas. Elderly men are more economically active than elderly women. These are very much predictable findings in the context of patriarchal socio-cultural milieu. However, it considerably adds to the vulnerability of the elderly women.

There are quite a few elderly women who are living with 'other than their natural family'. Let us then take a look at the occupational status of the head of such households, assuming that it may influence the vulnerability of the elderly women. Data show that among such heads of households, a large group (40 per cent) is of non-workers. Out of workers, 34 per cent are daily-wage earners and 32 per cent are agriculture workers. In a household, with meager income, due share given to elderly women for their upkeep, is a serious concern.

Income Distribution

Indeed, regular income is essential for meeting needs and maintaining the quality of life. It is often held that elderly women are, more or less, dependent on their family for their maintenance. Apparently, families with ample resources, most often, do not face a financial burden in caring for their aged. On the other hand, when household resources are scarce, youngsters invariably receive priority over the aged. As such, the socio-economic attributes of the household turn important in meeting the economic needs of elderly females and in shielding them from economic vulnerability. Let us take a close look at the income pattern.

Elderly women's income: Should elderly women have their own source of income, there is a good chance for them

Table 4.3: Respondents' and their Husband's Occupation (Percentage)

Occupation	*Respondent (Elderly Women)*			*Respondents' Husband*		
	Rural	*Urban*	*Total*	*Rural*	*Urban*	*Total*
Non-Worker/Housewife	60	60	60	39	41	40
Workers	40	40	40	61	59	60
Classification of Workers/Occupations						
Daily Wager	39	34	37	33	38	34
Agriculture Work	18	6	1	40	14	32
Business	8	14	10	13	24	16
Salaried Job	6	8	7	4	6	5
Pension	29	38	32	10	17	13
Total	**100**	**100**	**100**	**100**	**100**	**100**

to exercise considerable control over the situations influencing them. It would be relatively easy for them to maintain respect, status and security if they are financially self-reliant. However, Sarvekshana, (1991) reports that there are only 8.8 per cent females in rural areas and 4.8 per cent in urban areas who are economically independent. The corresponding figures for males are 52 per cent and 46 per cent. This suggests that economic vulnerability of elderly women is graver than their male counterparts. What is the situation in the present study?

Table 4.4: Respondents' Monthly Income by Occupation (N = 2935) (Percentage)

Occupation	*Low* (*Rs. 50-250*)	*Medium* (*Rs. 250-500*)	*High* (*Rs. 500 +*)	*Total*
Daily Wager	16	47	37	100
Agriculture Work	14	32	54	100
Business	20	36	44	100
Salaried Job	12	40	47	100
Pension	64	22	14	100
Total	**32**	**35**	**33**	**100**

Note: 62% elderly women do not earn income or non-workers.

Data of the present study show (Table 4.04) that only 40 per cent of the elderly women have some income of their own. It ranges from Rs. 50 to Rs. 8000 a month with wide variations. Mean value of respondents' income is Rs. 567 (standard deviation = 689). To facilitate analysis, monthly income of the elderly women has been divided into three groups — low income (less than Rs. 250), medium income (Rs. 251-500) and high income (more than Rs. 500). Table 4.05 shows the income of elderly women in terms of their occupation. It is found that the highest proportion of elderly women getting pension are in the category of low income. Daily wagers and salaried elderly women are generally having 'medium income'. Majority of women in agriculture work and salaried job are in the category of 'high income'.

Table 4.5: State-wise distribution of income pattern of elderly women (Percentage)

Income	*Low (Rs. 50-250)*	*Medium (Rs. 251-500)*	*High (Rs. 500 & +)*
Uttar Pradesh	22	39	39
Bihar	55	28	17
Jharkhand	27	31	42
Madhya pradesh	25	25	50
Chhattisgarh	26	44	30
Orissa	46	29	25
Assam	45	14	41
Sikkim	13	62	25
Total	**33**	**34**	**33**

Further, it would be beneficial to look into state-wise comparison of income patterns of elderly respondents. Table 4.05 shows that Bihar has the highest proportion of elderly respondents with low monthly income and is followed by Orissa and Assam. Sikkim and Assam, though are neighbouring states, share a wide gap in the proportion of elderly women with low income.

Pension is a source of income for quite a few elderly. Let us take a close look in the present study sample. Data show that 13 per cent of the elderly women get pension. Coming to the amount of pension, it was found to range from 61 rupees to 10,000 rupees (Mean = Rs. 1389; SD = 1535). For further analysis, amount of pension is divided into two groups — small (Rs. 100-150) and adequate (Rs. 501-10,000). Four per cent of the respondents are getting 'small' amount as pension and another four per cent women are getting large amount of pension. Rest of the respondents did not disclose their pension amount.

In the same connection, when asked about them receiving provident fund, gratuity, etc., only three per cent of the elderly women have responded in the affirmative. They have utilised these retirement benefits in marriage of children, construction of house, meeting medical expenses, children's career, education and initiating some income-generating programme. Only seven respondents (0.1 per cent) have kept the amount in safe custody to be appropriated suitably in future.

Husband's Income

Traditionally married aged women first look at their husband to meet their economic needs, then towards their progeny. It is, therefore, imperative to appraise the husbands' income. In the study, the range of income earned by elderly women's husbands is from Rs. 100 to Rs. 9000 a month. Average income is Rs.1314 (values of median and mode, 1000). The data are widely dispersed (standard deviation = 1240). There are 32 per cent elderly males with low earnings (Rs.100-600), another 34 per cent have medium income (Rs. 650-1300) and rest of the 33 per cent have income (Rs. 1400 and above). As a logical corollary, among the elderly men who were on salaried job, 83 per cent are earning high income. The second highest proportion of income (50 per cent) is from pension. Agriculture work provides lowest proportion of income.

Husband's strong financial position can make an elderly lady feel economically secure as would be seen from the case history given below:

Case History 4.2
Economically Secure

Godavari Devi, aged 70 years, lives with her husband in a joint family group. Well-settled in life, her two married daughters live separately. Her husband is 10th pass and has retired as a government teacher. He gets a monthly pension of Rs. 5000. Besides, he looks after farming which also yields the additional income of about sixty thousand a year.

On retirement, Godavari's husband received a sumptuous amount as PF, gratuity, etc. which was promptly utilised for renovating the ancestral house and for buying a used car. Both of her sons have migrated to Delhi and are in private job. Their wives and children are staying with the elderly couple. The family members are affectionate to her. She feels secure and contented.

Family income

It would be relevant to estimate total monthly income of the family of the elderly women under study. Data show (Diagram 4.1) a wide range of the monthly income of the family that is from Rs. 50 to Rs. 80,000. Average monthly income, however, is Rs. 2697. As would be expected, the data are highly heterogeneous (standard deviation = 3309).

Diagram 4.1

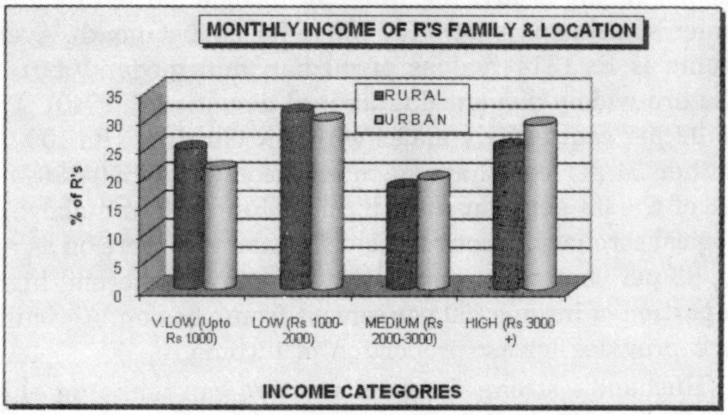

Diagram 4.1 shows a mild trend that income of elderly women's family is somewhat higher than their sisters in rural areas.

To facilitate analysis, total monthly income of the family has been divided into two groups based on poverty line. Taking the national average of family monthly income below poverty line as Rs.1700 in rural areas and Rs. 2300 in urban areas, families of respondents have been divided into two categories: family's monthly income as below poverty line (BPL) and above poverty line (APL).

Table 4.6 provides information on state, location and BPL and APL households. In general, data give the impression that majority of the families of respondents in rural as well as in urban areas belong to BPL families.

Table 4.6: Monthly Family Income of Respondents (Percentage)

State	*Rural*			*Urban*		
	BPL (> Rs. 1700)	*APL (< Rs. 1700)*	*Total*	*BPL (>Rs. 2300)*	*APL (<Rs 2300)*	*Total*
Assam	36	64	100	15	50	100
Bihar	67	33	100	77	23	100
Chhattisgarh	45	55	100	66	34	100
Jharkhand	57	43	100	49	51	100
Madhya Pradesh	39	61	100	45	55	100
Orissa	51	49	100	69	31	100
Sikkim	33	67	100	38	62	100
Uttar Pradesh	43	57	100	54	46	100
Total	**46**	**54**	**100**	**56**	**44**	**100**

The Table shows that Bihar, rural as well as urban, tops the list of BPL families. In urban Bihar situation is much worse. This largely conforms to national estimates.

The table further brings out that poverty in urban areas is more prominent in almost all the states. In rural areas, Jharkhand and Orissa, along with Bihar have more than a half of the families below poverty line. In urban areas, Assam, Sikkim, Madhya Pradesh and Jharkhand are the only states where families of respondents below poverty line are less than a half. In general, data give the impression that majority of the families of respondents are economically strained. Given this situation, do elderly women get their due share of resources to satisfy their basic needs?

Case History 4.3

Is old age a curse?

Sixty-five year old Ghoki Bibi is Muslim, but belongs to BC/OBC. With indifferent health and repeated bouts of illness, she looks thin and weak. Her clothes are usually dirty and frayed. She is illiterate. Although her husband is very much alive, he is bed-ridden. She is lucky to be receiving Old Age Pension. She makes some extra income by working as maid-servant, after she is free from taking care of her disabled husband.

Ghoki has three sons and a daughter — all married and live separately. Her house is just a small hut. The children hardly have time to care for their old parents. She had a piece of land that was sold off to get her husband's limb operated. However, now, she doesn't have money to continue the treatment. She has to make a tough choice between spending money over treatment and having three meals a day.

Economic Assets

Needless to mention, the possession of economic assets gives security and confidence to the possessor. These are also a source of income; and in varying degrees augment family budget. There is yet another angle to it. In old age, the ownership of movable and immovable property also seems to influence care giving in the family. In the simplest terms, if property is owned and is at the disposal of the elderly, care may be provided, in many instances, primarily with the expectation of inheritance. Let us examine the situation of immovable property in the family of elderly women.

Nine out of every ten elderly women affirm that their family has such immovable property as house, shop, orchard, land, and the like and ten per cent inform that they do not possess any immovable property. Rest of them remains silent on this issue. Nearly 90 per cent of the elderly women report that the family owns immovable property. What is the approximate value of the property? Table 4.7 gives the details of location wise value of immovable property possessed by the respondents' family.

The value of immovable family property ranges from Rs. 1000 to Rs. 16 lakhs, with wide variations (mean value, Rs.112653; and standard deviation, 148900). Immovable property is divided, in terms of value, into four groups—small (1000-

3000), modest (3000-60000), large (60000-125000) and very large (125000-1600000).

Table 4.7: Immovable Family Property's Value (Percentage)

Property's Value	*Rural*	*Urban*	*Total*
Small (Rs. 1000-3000)	4	2	4
Modest (Rs. 3000-60000)	49	46	48
Large (Rs. 60000-125000)	22	27	24
V. Large (125000-1600000)	24	25	24
Total	**100**	**100**	**100**

Does immovable property make for 'profitable asset'? We need to take a look at income, if any, from the immovable property. In this case too, range is very wide, from Rs. 60 to Rs. 75,000 a month. Data are highly heterogeneous (Mean = 2647; standard deviation = 7293). Monthly income from immovable property is divided into three groups — Small (60-1000, 15 per cent), adequate (1000-2000, 6.4 per cent) and substantial (2000-75000, 5.7 per cent). In the remaining cases no information has been furnished.

When specially asked about having immovable property in their own name, only 17 per cent respondents confirm this. The emphasis on the cultural tradition make women identify themselves with their family and hardly think about their independent income or space. Data bring out that there is slightly higher proportion of rural elderly women possessing property than their urban counterparts. Results further show that the title of immovable property in the name of elderly women is a rarity and that proportion of widow/unmarried/divorced women in having ownership of property is far larger than the currently married aged ladies.

Jewellery

In a society where the women commonly do not play an active role in financial transactions, possession of jewelry seems to give them a sense of importance and power. It is a traditional means of economic security. In old age, when a woman experiences change in her status and authority, ownership of silver, gold and diamond jewelry, to some extent, influences her 'bargaining power' in the family. In the study, only 28 per cent respondents have some jewelry with them (Average value Rs.7362.43). Looking at the value of jewelry, 15 per cent elderly have jewelry of modest value (Rs.100-2000) and 12 per cent of large value (Rs. 2000-800000). Rest of the elderly have not given any information on this issue.

Account in Bank/Post Office and Balance

Let us now take a look at the account of elderly women in bank or post office. Most of the elderly women (86 per cent) do not have any account in bank or post office. As many as 13 per cent respondents have an account in bank and one per cent elderly have that in post office.

Average amount in account is Rs. 5416 (Standard Deviation = 16441). The balance in account is divided into three — small (Rs. 50-500), modest (Rs. 501-1800) and large (Rs. 2000-30000). Data show that five per cent have small account, two per cent have medium and three per cent have large account. Does possession of jewelry and other assets ensure security and comfortable life?

Other Sources of Income

Apart from the income through occupation, pension or immovable/movable property, there may be other sources of income as well that help elderly women meet their needs. Data, in this regard, show that 15 per cent respondents receive money from their sons or relatives not staying with them.

When asked about any other sources of income, 95 per cent women respond in negative. Rest are involved in a wide range of activities, but at a very small scale. These are poultry, dairy, fishery, sericulture, horticulture, handicrafts, candle-making, *papad*-making, *bindi*-pasting, *masala*-packing, bangle shop, *bidi*-making, piggery, general store, etc. There are only a handful of elderly women who do not have any source of income, but still they are getting support from the community as would seen in the case of Ashiya:

Case History 4.4

Dependent on Fitra and Zakat

Ashiya is a 70 years old widow who sustains herself through begging in the village where she lives. Her husband was a daily wage worker. He died almost 30 years back. Her in-laws would not look after her, she came back to her parents' place with her only daughter. All the relatives ignored and neglected them. Then, about ten years back her daughter also died. Parents too were gone away from the scene. She was all-alone. She generally stays with her cousin but cooks separately. She has several health problems — cataract, blood pressure, digestive upsets and bronchitis. Village people collect *fitra and Zakat* and pass them on to her. This is the other source of income Ashiya has.

Expenditure Pattern

Let us pay attention to expenditure pattern among elderly women in the study.

Payment to Household: Reportedly, elderly women give money for their maintenance in the family. Aged women giving some amount to the family for their up keep are expected to have the feeling of security. On the other hand, aged women who do not or cannot pay anything may have a feeling of dependency, which in turn, seems to have negative impact on their feeling of security and well-being. Most of the elderly women (74 per cent) do not pay anything for their upkeep in the household. Another 23 per cent respondents pay some amount per month to their family for their up keep.

Monthly Expenditure: No reliable analysis can be made of the income of a person unless expenditure pattern is taken into account. In this study, an attempt is made to get at the expenditure pattern in the family on various heads like food, clothing, education, etc. Table 4.8 presents state-wise details of monthly expenditure patterns in the families of the respondents. It shows that there is a consistency in expenditure on food but Assam, Bihar and Chhattisgarh have a little lower expenditure on food. On clothing, women in Assam are spending

Table 4.8: Average Monthly Estimated Family Expenses (in Rupees)

State	*Food*	*Clothing*	*Conv-eyance*	*Medic-ine*	*Edu-cation*	*Gifts/ Donation*	*Total Exp.*	*Percentage of Total R*
Assam	458	100	42	45	58	26	729	14
Bihar	781	153	121	159	131	48	1393	10
Chhattisgarh	742	218	108	118	159	68	1414	10
Jharkhand	1084	218	98	111	272	69	1842	14
Madhya Pradesh	1499	158	95	104	300	76	2232	13
Orissa	1280	228	190	151	249	131	2230	13
Sikkim	1435	216	126	160	332	96	2365	13
Uttar Pradesh	1023	290	172	205	244	99	2034	13
Total	**1046**	**199**	**115**	**129**	**244**	**75**	**1808**	**100**
% Share	**58**	**11**	**6**	**7**	**14**	**4**	**100**	

the least and those in Uttar Pradesh the most. Conveyance forms the lowest proportion of family budget in Assam while elderly women in Uttar Pradesh and Orissa are spending the most. Women of Assam again spend least amount on medicine.

Further, expenditure on education of children/grandchildren is least in Assam and most in Sikkim. Also, elderly women in Orissa are spending almost five times more money on buying gifts for relatives/donations than their counterparts in Assam. The reason may be traced back to certain religious-cultural practices, as also to resource availability.

Expenditure Held Up: At times, certain expenditures are held up for want of money. Such situations tend to have a deleterious effect on the well-being of the aged women. Let us examine the situation in the study area.

Diagram 4.2

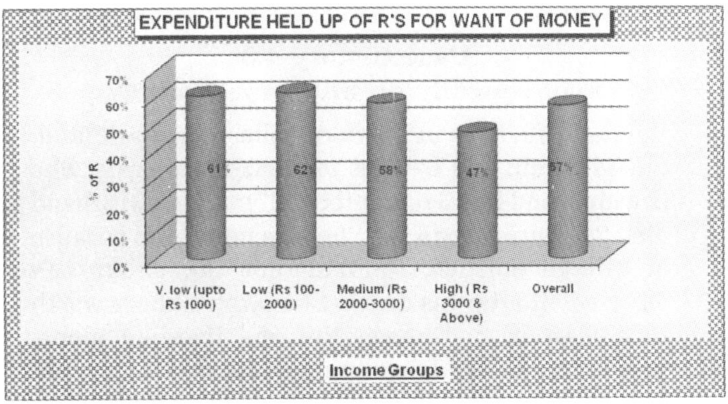

On asking whether any of their expenditures are held up for want of money, 57 per cent of the elderly women have replied in affirmative. There are many manifestations of this expenditure being held up. They are house needing repair, medical treatment being postponed, marriage of daughters, grandchildren, medical treatment of husband, etc. As would be expected this kind of situation, expenditure held-up for want of money is more with those family group, which have low income as shown in Diagram 4.2. Below are the two case histories, highlighting the shortage of money to meet certain needs.

Case History 4.5
Economically Insecure

Rahima Khatun is 65 Years. She is an illiterate Muslim widow. She lives in perpetual destitution in the city of Tezpur. She has no close relatives to take care. She lives all alone in a dilapidated thatched hut.

Her main problem is isolation. Her sons left her after getting married and almost forgot about her. For want of money, she is not able to fulfill her basic needs. She works as a maid servant in her locality. She gets Rs. 200 from a relative as help. Besides she receives Rs. 75 per month as Old Age Pension. Somehow Rahima manages herself but finds it difficult to have medical treatment, the amount she gets is hardly sufficient even for as daily necessities.

Case History 4.6
Economically on Slippery Grounds

Ramkali, 70, lives in Tinsukia village in Jharkhand. She is Hindu and belongs to a backward caste. She is widow and has 3 daughters, all married. Husband died 20 years ago; in fact, he was murdered because of village politics. Ramkali got the daughter's married off after his death. She owns a house worth Rs.4 lakh in her name. But she lives all alone. Besides one of her daughters send Rs. 600 per month. The house badly needs repair. It is likely to cost much and she has neither money nor energy.

Sense of Security

Security means safety and freedom from danger or anxiety. Does the sense of security only depend on the financial position of the aged? D' Souza (1990) brings out those aged who are economically dependent on their children often suffer from tension and anxiety. Soodan (1975) highlights that in old age economic stringency brings insecurity and loss of social status. These studies show that age, children, financial position and economic dependence are associated with the feeling of economic security-insecurity.

In the present study, economic security is the confidence of an elderly woman that she would get money whenever she needs. Her family would come forward to help her as and when required. In order to measure the feeling of economic security insecurity, elderly women have been asked whether they feel they can get money as per their needs or wishes, say, for buying fruits, confectionary, for their medical treatment, etc.

Data show that 27 per cent of the elderly women feel that they could buy clothes whenever they want to do so. Similarly, 46 per cent feel that they could spend money on giving doles, according to their will. On medical treatment, 14 per cent respondents feel that they could spend big amounts if the need arises. Further, 49 per cent elderly feel that their family members willingly meet their expenses.

Income-Generating Programme

In the study, elderly women were asked about their interest in income generating activities. This not only gives them additional money, but also affords them a sense of fulfillment. It would be seen one out of every six women (17 per cent) is interested in doing some income generating activities as shown in Table 4.9. In this regard, there is a hardly any notable difference between those who live in rural or urban area. This apart, it would be interesting to see as to what are the income generating activities, preferred by the elderly women.

Type of activities	*Rural*	*Urban*	*Total*
Yes, but not specify	52%	45%	50%
Tailoring, Stitching, Embroidery etc.	1%	2%	1%
Training Centre for Stitching and Tailoring	2%	0%	2%
Poultry	3%	3%	3%
Dairy	5%	4%	5%
Goatery	1%	1%	1%
Piggery	0%	0%	0%
Fishery	2%	3%	2%
Sericulture	2%	0%	1%
Horticulture	2%	1%	1%

Type of activities	*Rural*	*Urban*	*Total*
Handicrafts	4%	3%	3%
Candle and Paper Work	2%	5%	3%
Papad Making	2%	1%	1%
Bindi Paste Work	3%	3%	3%
Agarbatti Making	3%	3%	3%
Bidi Making	0%	2%	1%
General Store	6%	8%	6%
Fruits Shop	2%	5%	3%
Vegetable Shop	3%	2%	3%
Masala Packing	2%	4%	3%
Bangle Shop	0%	2%	1%
Pots Shop	1%	1%	1%
Running Hotel	1%	2%	1%
Garage Work	0%	2%	1%
Coaching Centre	1%	1%	1%
Total	**100%**	**100%**	**100%**

Table 4.9 provides details of different income generating activities; the elderly women are interested in. Among them who showed their interest in income generating activities, almost a half have not specified any activity. Rest of the respondents have expressed desire to take up such activities as poultry, dairy, and the like. Almost an equal proportion of women are interested in grocery shop, vegetable, fruit shop, hotel, etc.

The respondents were further asked about the type of assistance required to initiate income-generating activities. Majority of the elderly women (63 per cent) require financial assistance. About seven per cent need technical know-how and market linkages. Rest of them do not require any help.

There are many factors that make elderly women economically vulnerable. Patriarchal social structure often discourages economic self-reliance among women. In old age, dependence on others accentuates their vulnerability. In Chapter Eight, a composite variable economic vulnerability, would be dealt with in detail. Here it may be mentioned that economic vulnerability tends to vary with the marital status of the elderly women, as would be seen from diagram 4.3.

Diagram 4.3

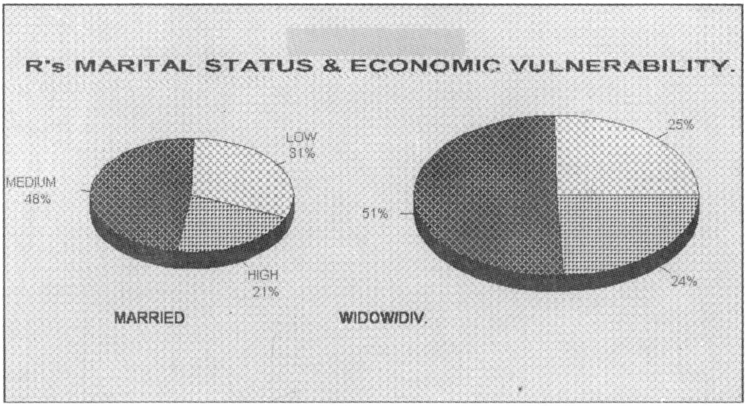

Divorced, widowed and separated elderly women are relatively more economically vulnerable for understandable reasons.

The foregoing account brings out that a large proportion of the elderly women face economic stringency. They have diminutive income. More than six out of every ten elderly women, whether from rural areas or urban areas are 'below the poverty line'. Quite a few live on alms. And the proportion of those whose essential expenditures are held up for want of money is large. What is mere, very many among them suffer from a sense of (economic) insecurity. Assuredly, they require income-generation programmes suited to physical and mental process.

5

Nutrition and Health

Ageing is generally taken as the accumulation of degenerative and deteriorative changes that occur with age in life. Indeed, these changes are essentially irreversible. The natural process of ageing is associated with a decline in body's strength and vigour and decreasing sensory and functional abilities. Ageing makes the body vulnerable to deterioration and eventual death. Kirkwood (1988) observes that human body has an 'in-built programme' to decay and die in order to make way for younger members of the species, preventing overcrowding, which is termed as 'programmed senescence'.

In this process of ageing, tissues, such as the skin and muscles, become less elastic. Urinary system becomes slower and less efficient in excreting toxins and other waste-products, leading to a number of kidney-related problems. The gastrointestinal system reduces enzyme-secretion resulting in digestive upsets. There is decline in muscle-mass and strength, which may give rise to certain locomotor infirmities. The respiratory system takes in less oxygen leading to decrease in vigour (see Hamilton, 1994). Aiken (1989) observes that an average 75 year-old person's cardiac-output is, approximately, 70 per cent of the average 50 year-old individual's. In old age, the cardiovascular system suffers a double blow — the heart decreases in strength and, simultaneously, arteries get hardened and shrunk making pumping of blood around the body more energy-consuming. In old age, there may be certain obvious changes in mental faculties, similar to ones at the physiological level. In brain, the cells become weaker as cerebral blood flow decreases, thereby less oxygen is available to the neurons.

This somewhat reduces efficiency of the brain leading to delays in learning new things and creative thinking, poor recent memories but better remote memories, mental rigidity, tendency to reminiscing and forgetfulness (Hurlock, 1976).

However, even though, in old age, body does become susceptible to a number of illnesses, yet this does not mean that ageing is synonymous to disease or illness. It implies that the criterion of 'being healthy' differs and should differ in different stages of human life-cycle including old-age.

Health and Elderly Women

It is often held that 'women are sicker but men die sooner'. Epidemiologically, apart from age-related ailments like diabetes, hypertension, deterioration in sensory capabilities, etc., females suffer from two broad health disorders, gynaecological and postmenopausal morbidities.

Certain socio-cultural factors also add to the morbidity among females. All through the life-cycle, females are subject to various kinds of discrimination, oppression and exploitation. Parents' preference for male-child, right from birth to educational and health facilities, nutrition and other resource-allocation, early marriage, multiple pregnancies are some factors accumulated effects of which contribute to vulnerability of may gynaecological complications and nutritional deficiencies, fastening the ageing deterioration among females (Bagchi, 1997).

Nutrition

Elderly persons are at a greater risk of malnourishment due to reasons more than one. Depletion in purchasing power affects nutrition and, in turn, health of people thereby making them susceptible to accelerated ageing. Economic hardship poses hurdles in maintaining optimum standards of food.

In old age, absorption and digestion capacity of the body declines, teeth decay and chewing becomes difficult which leads to nutritional vulnerability. There is lack of knowledge about proper dietary intake. Also, the issue of nutritional needs of the elderly has been largely ignored. Elderly people often require special diet due to certain restrictions of food options, diminished taste acuity, faulty denture and many times caregivers are not in a position to adhere to prescribed dietary patterns.

Diseases like diabetes, high/low blood pressure, arthritis, osteoporosis, etc., often limit many types of food-intake. It may result in malnourishment, especially of vitamins and minerals, which, in turn, add to the risk of various nutritional disorders and ailments. To combat decreasing body strength, an elderly person requires nutritious diet. However, a number of factors mentioned above pose hurdles to the availability, consumption and absorption of many food items. All these factors seem to add to nutritional vulnerability of elderly persons.

Coming to gender issues, malnutrition has been a way of life for most Indian women. Since childhood they have learnt to be last in having meals in the family and that too many times, just the 'left over'. Repeated and many pregnancies take heavy toll of their health. Menopause brings in osteoporosis that among others, degenerates bones. Several gynæcological problems also crop up. With interplay of all these factors, old age increases frequency of morbidity among elderly women.

Healthy Habits: Health

Health is considered the biggest wealth. Gerontologists are advocating active ageing for elderly, which calls for adopting and maintaining healthy habits and life-style for quality life in golden years. Balanced diet, light exercise, yoga and relaxation are recommended for the elderly to live a healthy life.

Activities of Daily Living

Personal autonomy is one of the indicators of quality of life in old age. It is, generally, achieved through good health-condition, proper exercise and adequate diet. Self-dependence in Activities of Daily Living (ADL) play crucial role in the life-style of an aged. Dependence on others for daily life activities not only brings in misery but also decreases confidence and self-esteem among the elderly. It tends to increase vulnerability among the elderly. What is the situation in the present study?

Table 5.1: Daily Life Activities of Elderly Women (Percentage)

Daily life Activities	*At My Own*	*Require Some Help*	*Total*
Eating	98	2	100
Bathing/ Dressing	94	6	100
Walking	94	6	100
Getting up & sitting	95	5	100
Kitchen Work	44	56	100
Taking Medicines/Pills	87	13	100
Washing/Laundering	51	49	100

In the present study, majority of elderly women (Table 5.1) are independent in doing most of their daily life activities like bathing and dressing, getting up and sitting, walking, etc. There are a few elderly women (2 per cent) who require help in eating. These women are among the most dependent and vulnerable. Most of the elderly women require some help in kitchen work. Panda (2005) finds that with increasing age there is reduction in autonomy in ADL. Dependence in ADL tends to increase vulnerability.

Exercise and Recreation

Healthy habits like balanced diet with timings, light exercise, adequate sleep, involvement in household activities, and the like go a long way in maintaining 'active and healthy ageing' (see Khan 1997). Let us look at some of such habits that help the elderly living a healthy life. It may be assumed that getting up early in the morning helps in several ways and has a positive impact on the health of a person. In the study, most of the elderly women (92 per cent) are early risers, that is, they get up within thirty minutes of sun-up. Another four per cent elderly women reported to be late risers (one hour after sun-up). Coming to duration of sleep, most of the women are found to have adequate sleep (six hours or more) and very few complain of inadequate sleep (less than six hours).

The elderly undertake several activities to keep themselves healthy. In the study, respondents have been asked what they do to keep themselves fit. It is found that 84 per cent of the respondents do not do anything specific. There are 14 per cent elderly women who go for morning or evening walk for keeping themselves fit. Two per cent elderly do light exercise or yoga for maintaining health.

Healthy Habits: Nutrition

Nutrition is crucial for a healthy and active life-style. However, as discussed above, elderly women have far greater chances of nutritional vulnerability. Towards this, eating patterns and habits, being vegetarian or non-vegetarian, go a long way in ensuring nutritional and health status of elderly women. In the study, 34 per cent elderly women are vegetarian and 66 per cent of them non-vegetarian. Cultural dimensions play a very important role in food habits of a person.

Study results show that Assam is a predominantly non-vegetarian state (91 per cent elderly women of Assam are non-vegetarian) and Orissa (87 per cent) comes the next followed by Sikkim (79 per cent) and Jharkhand (75 per cent). Madhya Pradesh has maximum proportion of vegetarian elderly women (67 per cent) followed by Uttar Pradesh (54 per cent). In Bihar 58 per cent and in Chhattisgarh 56 per cent of elderly women are non-vegetarian. Thus, states like Assam, Orissa, and Sikkim are essentially non-vegetarian. On the other hand, Madhya Pradesh and Uttar Pradesh are predominantly vegetarian. It is general observation, though with many exceptions, that in most of the eastern and north-eastern states, food pattern of majority of citizens is non-vegetarian while people in northern states prefer vegetarian food. As is well known, food preferences or taboos often differ with religion. Results show that most Muslims (nearly 90 per cent) are non-vegetarian as compared to about 60 per cent of the Hindu elderly women. What is the impact of food preference on the health status of elderly women? This dimension would be dealt further in subsequent sections of the report.

Let us take a look at the nutritional status of elderly women in the study. Carbohydrates are the main source of energy for human body. They help basic functioning of the body. The elderly women have been asked to describe about their dietary intake on the preceding day (See table 5.2). In

Table 5.2: Distribution of type and quantity of food intake among respondents during last day (Percentage)

Food item	*Did not have*	*Adequate Intake*	*Somewhat Inadequate Intake*	*Inadequate Intake*
Chapati, rice	3	90	6	1.0
Fish	89	7	2	0.1
Eggs, meat	89	8	2	0.1
Milk, milk products	65	27	7	0.3
Green vegetables	26	59	14	0.8
Fruits	87	9	2	0.3

terms of intake of chapati, rice, etc., majority has had adequate quantity. There are about three per cent respondents who could not have even staple diet.

Analysis of the data presented in the table show that majority of the elderly women are not taking nutritious diet and intake of proteins is lacking both between the vegetarian and non-vegetarian women. Further, fruit intake — a major source of vitamins and minerals — also lacks among elderly women. Green leafy vegetables should also find a place in the meals of the aged. About 26 per cent of respondents did not have vegetables. In old age, body loses its strength and vigour and if the elderly do not have balanced diet, this enhances their vulnerability. Lack of knowledge as well as resources are usually responsible for malnourishment among the elderly.

Data gathered through Focus Group Discussions show that poverty and lack of adequate resources make it difficult for the grown up children to provide adequate nutrition for their elderly parents. This was particularly evident in Madhubani district of Bihar and Goalpara of Assam. One official, during FGD states, that there are only 20 per cent women who get meals thrice a day, rest of them are too poor for it. A senior medical officer of Sonitpur (in Assam) had similar observations to make — in urban areas 40 per cent of elderly women are getting nutritious food and 60 per cent of them are still deprived of it.

A senior officer of the ICDS reports that most of the elderly ladies get stale food and hardly have adequate quantity of food. The ICDS officer asserts that many of them live on leftover food. Contrary to this, a few elderly women said that since they do not require nutritious diet especially milk and milk products, they give these items to their grandchildren. The Block Development Officer at Cuttack maintains that natural calamities like flood affect food availability in many districts of Orissa and elderly are the worst affected in such situations. Likewise, in Goalpara, many officials maintain that as many as 30 per cent of Assamese elderly women do not get nutritious diet. Many officials and NGO workers state that, at times, elderly women have awareness about nutritious diet but still they do not have it.

Apparently poverty is the main cause of deficient dietary intake and poor nutritional status of the elderly, but equally important in this regard is nutrition awareness. Most elderly women lack knowledge about nutritious food and those who are aware even they do not ensure intake of balanced diet. Socio-cultural practices of women eating at the end and beliefs that 'females' do not require nutritious diets add to nutritional vulnerability among elderly women.

Health Problems: Physical

Usually old age brings in many health problems due to certain irreversible anatomical and physiological changes. This apart, present-day life-style, characterised by imbalanced nutrition, lack of exercise, more or less constant stress, tension and no time for relaxation and enjoyment, are major factors of non-communicable diseases like heart problem, arthritis, diabetes, hypertension, etc. Let us take a close look at the situation of elderly women in the study.

Sensory Capabilities

With advancing age, the capacity of the sensory organs

deteriorates. Hamilton (1994) observes that lens of the eye loses elasticity leading to *presbiopia* (long sightedness).

Table 5.3: Distribution of sensory capabilities among elderly women (Percentage)

Sensory Capabilities	*Unchanged*	*Gone Down*
Vision	21.1	78.4
Bones/joints	29.7	70.3
Hearing	54.0	46.0
Psychomotor	71.4	28.6

Hearing impairment also begin to crop up and *presbycusis* (loudness recruitment) may develop. In the study, data show that most of the elderly women have experienced deterioration in sensory capabilities (See table 5.3). Most affected are vision and bone joints.

Analysis shows that declining vision is the most common sensory problem followed by problems of bones and joints, which directly impacts. On the persons' locomotion. It is further seen that elderly women in villages are comparatively better off than their sisters in town and cities (Values of Pearson's R for vision=0.23; hearing: 0.21; locomotion=0.27; psychomotor= 0.20). Thus hardly speaks well of urban medical facilities.

Analysis shows that declining hearing is a more common sensory problem than psychomotor reactions. It is observed that elderly women in urban areas are relatively healthier in this regard than those in rural area (See also diagram 5.1). Could this be attributed to better urban medical facilities?

Diagram 5.1

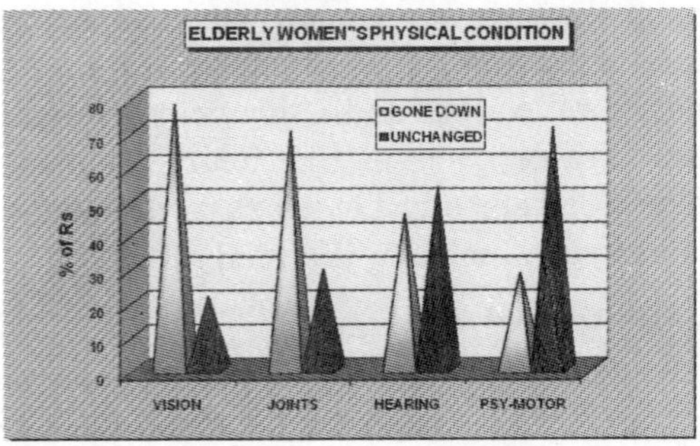

Medical Complaints

It is a common observation that elderly women have several medical complaints. Table 5.4 reflects upon the medical complaints of the respondents.

Table 5.4: Medical Complaints among the Respondents (Percentage)

Medical Complaints	*Having Problem*
Blood Pressure	20
Heart Problem	10
Gynecological	4
Sugar/Diabetes	4
Digestive Upset	29
Prolonged Coughing	29
Stones	2
Liver/Jaundice	2

It is observed that digestive upsets and prolonged coughing or breathing problems are the most common medical complaints. Contrary to other studies, (see Panda, 2005; Ganesh, 2004), quite a few elderly women are found suffering from gynaecological problems. This apart, there is a wide range of medical complaints reported by elderly women in the study. These include: general weakness, malaria, fever, back pain, thyroid, filaria, anaemia, tonsils, paralysis, etc.

Physical Disability

Apart from physical impairments (three per cent) quite a few elderly persons suffer from a variety of physical disability. The aging body often reduces its ability to recover fast due to a number of anatomical and physiological reasons. It reduces autonomy and is quite stressful for the caregivers too.

In the study, 257 elderly women (three per cent) are suffering from one disability or another. Among these disabled elderly women, most (54 per cent) are visually handicapped, 23 per cent have hearing difficulties and 14 per cent have locomotion disability.

Table 5.5: Type of Disability (Percentage)

State	Percentage of Disabled Respondents	Type of Disability					
		Visual (Blind)	Hearing	Speech	H and S*	Locomotor	Mental
Assam	6	69	22	0	0	9	0
Bihar	4	47	19	3	0	17	14
Chhattisgarh	3	42	13	8	0	29	8
Jharkhand	3	54	43	0	0	4	0
Madhya Pradesh	5	65	12	0	2	13	8
Orissa	2	53	11	16	11	11	0
Sikkim	3	42	31	4	0	23	0
Uttar Pradesh	2	28	44	6	0	17	6
Total	3	54	23	3	1	14	5

* HS=Hearing and Speech.

Turning attention to the study states, largest proportion of elderly women were suffering from disability in Assam (six per cent) followed by Madhya Pradesh (five per cent) and Bihar (four per cent). Chhattisgarh, Jharkhand and Sikkim have three per cent of disabled elderly women in each. Uttar Pradesh and Orissa have the least proportion of disabled elderly women — two per cent each. Are there any specific services for disabled elderly women?

During Focus Group Discussions, many officials maintained that poverty and lack of nutritious diet lead to many disabilities. These are largely preventable but, due to ignorance and lack of timely health care services, often permanent handicaps.

Mental Health Complaints

Mental health problems like anxiety and tension are quite common especially among the elderly. WHO (1996) observes that about 90 million persons in India would be suffering from major clinical depression at some stage in their life. It indicates the gravity of mental health problems among elderly women.

Diagram 5.2 deals with such mental problems as anxiety/ tension, sleeplessness, and mental pressure and depression among the elderly women. The trend is that these problems are severe in the category of old-old. Mental health complaints like tension and stress have serious repercussion on the physical, mental and social well-being of a person.

Diagram 5.2

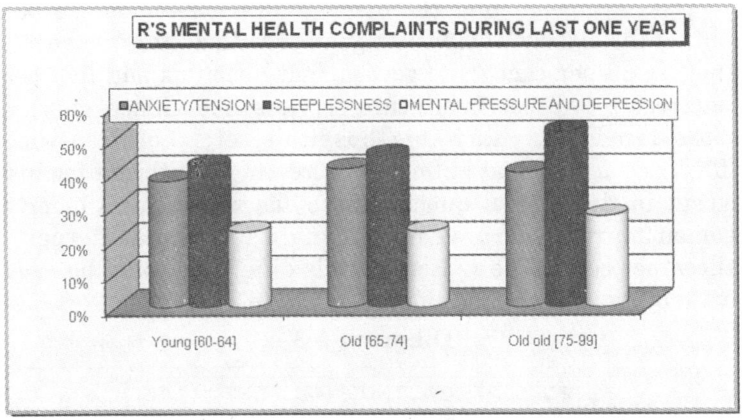

In most cases, problems go unnoticed. Often a lot of stigma is attached to mental health problems as society, community and families have a very conservative and biased attitude towards persons suffering from any mental ailments. In turn, the problems get aggravated.

It would be relevant to examine mental health complaints in terms of the states under study. It is seen that sleeplessness is a quite common problem (45 per cent) among elderly women, followed by anxiety/tension (40 per cent) and mental pressure and depression (23 per cent). It is found that the state of Assam has the highest number of elderly women, who are under anxiety/tension (72 per cent), followed by Chhattisgarh (64 per cent) and Uttar Pradesh (50 per cent). In terms of insomnia or sleeplessness, Assam again figures prominently (62 per cent), followed by Uttar Pradesh (55 per cent) and Jharkhand (50 per cent). Uttar Pradesh is prominent (32 per cent) in terms of mental pressure among the elderly women.

Hospitals: Availability and Accessibility

As is well known the country has a network of medical facilities. In the government sector we have PHCs, CHCs, District hospitals, regional hospitals and teaching hospitals. Besides we have private clinics, nursing homes and hospitals. In certain rural and urban areas quacks and ojhas also practise. Where do the elderly women go to when ailing?

Data bring out that there are almost one-fourth (26 per cent) of the elderly women who go to private doctors/hospitals. Another 69 per cent go to government hospitals and five per cent resort to other healthcare services like village quacks, home remedies, charitable hospitals, etc. Location-wise difference is marginal in terms of accessing healthcare facility except in the case of quacks and ojhas where rural elderly women (six per cent) are double than their urban counterparts (three per cent). The reason for this difference could be easy availability of such traditional healers in rural areas.

Diagram 5.3

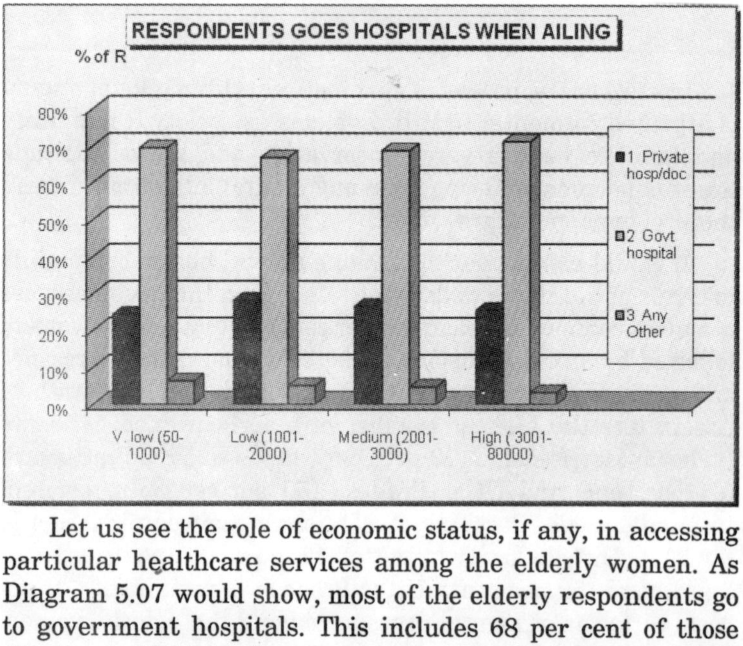

Let us see the role of economic status, if any, in accessing particular healthcare services among the elderly women. As Diagram 5.07 would show, most of the elderly respondents go to government hospitals. This includes 68 per cent of those who have high family income. On the other hand, private practitioners and hospitals are also found to have a substantial place in offering healthcare services to the elderly women.

How far is the nearest healthcare facility available to the elderly women? Data analysis shows that distance of nearest government hospital range is from one kilometer to fifty kilometers. Mean distance is about four kilometers. Data are quite heterogeneous (Standard Deviation = 4.3). For further analysis, distance to nearest government hospital is grouped into three: small distance (1-2 kilometers) and somewhat large distance (3-5 kilometers) and large distance (6-50 kilometers).

Table 5.6 brings the details of distance of nearest healthcare facility from the place of residence of elderly women. As expected, rural urban difference is quite visible in terms of availability of healthcare facility at the nearest distance. The proportion of elderly women in urban areas having government hospital within the radius of 1-2 kilometers is almost two and a half times than their rural counterparts. The situation is worse in the case of private hospitals. Urban areas more frequently have health facilities — whether private hospitals or government ones — at 'small' or 'somewhat small' distances while rural areas generally have these healthcare facilities at a large distance. With deplorable transportation facility, existence of healthcare facilities at large distance has graver consequences.

Table 5.6: Distance-Government and Private Hospitals

Distance	*Government Hospital*			*Private Hospital*		
	Rural	*Urban*	*Total*	*Rural*	*Urban*	*Total*
Small (1-2 kms)	32	73	45	26	71	40
Some What (3-5 kms)	40	20	34	29	11	24
Large (6 and above kms)	28	7	21	45	18	36
Total	**100**	**100**	**100**	**100**	**100**	**100**

As expected, accessibility both of government and private hospitals in urban areas is much easier for most of the elderly women while those in rural areas have to cover a large distance to reach to their nearest government/private hospital. This clearly shows that the health vulnerability of elderly women staying in rural areas, is likely to be high.

Since it is often difficult for the elderly to cover a long distance to reach to health care services, mobile vans came forward to provide basic medical treatment to the needy at their doorstep. In this regard, respondents were asked about mobile care services in their area. Data show that two per cent respondents confirmed that mobile van visits their area regularly and 98 per cent replied in the negative.

When asked about availing the services of mobile health unit, only a few replied in a affirmative and the rest maintained that they do not avail these services. Data show a marginal difference in rural-urban areas in terms of visit of mobile health units.

As part of health security for the elderly, regular medical camps are being organised by government as well as by the NGOs. In this context, elderly women were asked about medical camps being organised in their neighbourhood and utilisation of their services. About 16 per cent respondents state that medical camp was held during last one year in their area. Location-wise analysis shows that this facility is slightly more frequently available to urban elderly (20 per cent) than their rural counterparts (15 per cent). Further, only seven per cent of the respondents have availed these services.

Hospitalisation

For having a greater understanding of the health vulnerability among elderly women, they have been asked about their hospitalisation. Data show that 15 per cent of them have been admitted to a hospital during the last one year and there is only a slight difference in terms of elderly ladies who have undergone hospitalisation in urban (16 per cent) and rural areas (15 per cent).

Table 5.7: Admitted in Private or Government Hospitals (Percentage)

Type of Hospitals	*Rural*	*Urban*	*Total*
Nursing Home Hospitals	38	41	39
Government Hospital	60	55	58
Medical College	1	3	2
Any Other	1	1	1
Total	**100**	**100**	**100**

For hospitalisation, which type of facility, the elderly women have had? It is observed (Table 5.7) that 39 per cent went for private nursing home or hospitals while 58 per cent have preferred government hospitals. It is further observed that there are marked differences in rural and urban areas. Urban elderly women more often go to private hospitals while rural elderly women go to government hospitals. One of reasons may be of availability and accessibility. In rural areas, private hospitals are not frequently available. Stakeholders like Block Development Officers, Chief Medical Officers, also express similar opinion during focus group discussions.

Often treatment and patient care at private hospitals is considered better than in government hospitals. In the study, among those who received treatment during last one year, 38 per cent respondents rated treatment effectiveness as good, 52 per cent rated it as so-so or just right. In the same connection, 36 per cent respondents rated patient care in their respective health care setting as good, 55 per cent ranked it as so-so or just right. Data show marginal difference in rural and urban elderly women in rating treatment effectiveness and patient care. However, urban elderly women are more satisfied with treatment and care in health care settings than their rural counterparts.

In the study, 23 per cent respondents are taking medicine for one ailment or the other. The elderly women have been asked to give their opinion whether or not their family members meet their medical expenses willingly. Only 21 per cent of them feel that their families easily meet their medical expenses while 79 per cent feel otherwise. Results show that there is no difference in location in terms of caregivers' stress to meet medical expenses of their elderly relatives.

Medical insurance is one of the most important ingredients of health security among the elderly. However, in India, medical insurance is not very popular. In the case of women, there is a felt need to get medical insurance policy. Findings of the study reflect the same viewpoint. Only 63 elderly women (1 per cent), in the study, have medical insurance in their name. Data analysis informs that in Sikkim and Chhattisgarh not even a single elderly woman has medical insurance policy. More than 99 per cent respondents in almost all the states do not have medical policy in their name. Does it add to health vulnerability among elderly women?

Neglecting /Postponing Treatment

Many studies on the health seeking behaviour among females show that women, in general, tend to neglect and postpone their medical treatment. It is, therefore, hard to expect that in old age women promptly seek medical care when needed. Postponement of treatment results in multiplying gravity of medical problems and heavy cost of health and economic resources. Finding of the study show (Table 5.8) that 20 per cent of elderly women are postponing treatment for their ailments.

Table 5.8: Neglecting / Postponing Treatment (Percentage)

Age Category	*Yes*	*No*	*Total*
Young (60-64)	19	81	100
Old (65-74)	20	80	100
Old-Old (75-99)	21	79	100
Total	**20**	**80**	**100**

Age-wise data on postponement of treatment show that proportion of elderly women postponing treatment is similar in all age groups (see Table 5.8). Reasons given for postponing treatment are varied. Most frequently cited reason is lack of money as expressed by 40 per cent elderly women among those who are postponing the treatment. Secondly, two per cent feel that their treatment is not in the priority of family members or family members do not pay attention to their ailments and one per cent elderly women do not have anybody to care for them. Rest of the women preferred silence on this.

Possibility is strong that postponement of medical treatment by the elderly women may be related to their present income. This is what clearly comes out when we pay attention to diagram 5.8. Among those who have been postponing medical treatment and having low income, the proportion is as high as almost 46 per cent. In contrast, this proportion slides to 19 per cent in the case of medium and high income groups.

Diagram 5.4

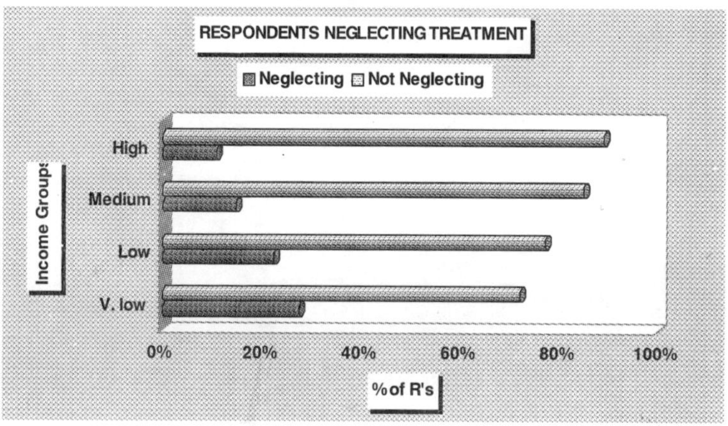

Health vulnerability among elderly women is significantly higher. In this chapter, we have attempted to explore various factors adding to or inhibiting nutritional and health vulnerability among the elderly women. We have observed that socio-cultural factors play crucial role in nutritional and health seeking behaviour. Added to this are issues of accessibility and affordability. In subsequent sections, impact of nutritional and health vulnerability on the overall vulnerability would be looked into.

6

Interpersonal Relations

Interpersonal relations form the crux of human life. The web of interpersonal relations is knit by social institutions like family and community, which provide a sense of belongingness, acceptance, security and recognition. The elderly are no exception to this. Interaction with family and significant others, involvement in community affairs, respect from youngsters brings a sense of acceptance and satisfaction among the aged (see: Stevens, 1992). Indeed, satisfying and harmonious interpersonal relations provide security and well-being to the elderly. However, when these relationships with family members and significant others become strained and incongruent, the elderly become vulnerable. Does old age change interpersonal relations of women with their family and community? Do age-related changes influence interpersonal relations? What is the impact of interpersonal relations on the social vulnerability of elderly women?

In may be restated that, in the agrarian society, the social situation was much favourable to the elderly that compensated for their increasing health vulnerability. The elderly as the Head of the household would control the family property. They were the decision-makers in family matters. Their knowledge was relevant to the then agrarian economy – they would tell youngsters when to sow seeds and how to do weeding. These factors not only ensured their economic security but also provided them high status and reverence.

In agrarian social system, among other, widely prevalent institution of joint-family proved to be a boon for the elderly.

Age and sex were the two defining principles of social status and position and, thus, there was very high and respectable position of the elderly, particularly, teachers, saints, family, clan, village and tribal heads, who would be old or even old.

It is, however, doubtful that aged women enjoyed same privileges, as did elderly men. Nevertheless, they would enjoy authority over the younger members of the household, especially the females. Their status would increase especially when their son brings home the *'bahu'*. They used to act as mediator, educator, doctor, and consultant in various day-to-day family matters. Also, they would play active role in the performance of cultural practices, rituals and obligations. They would be invariably consulted in matters related to childbirth and minor healthcare particularly of women and children, not only by females of the family but also in the neighborhood. They were often approached for matters related to kitchen work like pickle, *bari, chutney, papad* making, food preservation, etc. (Panda, 2005).

Added to this, elderly women would play important role in the socialisation of their grandchildren. Through story-telling, grandmothers, not only would provide recreational inputs but subtly help grandchildren in learning moral values. During religious and cultural ceremonies, for instance, *annaprassana* (rice eating ceremony) or functions associated with fixation and performance of marriage of grandchildren, the specifications and modalities given by the aged women were highly relevant and agrreable to all. Thus, the elderly women proved to be a useful link for transmission of traditional and cultural practices, values and ethos from the older to the younger generation. Their involvement in these activities helped them in social integration. All these salient roles played by the aged females contributed significantly to their acceptance in the family (see Kakkar, 1982; Jamuna, 1995).

In the agrarian social system, in absence of family support, for any reasons, it used to be the duty of the village-fellowmen to look after them. Also, community, often known as *biradary,* has had exerted considerable pressure on families to care for their elderly relatives by making it a code of conduct for younger family members (Singh, 1995). There used to be also a kind of unwritten code for the youngsters who would face social boycott and suffer a loss of prestige, should they fail in taking care of their elderly.

The social situation, in the contemporary world has undergone radical changes due to certain social forces like commercialisation, industrialisation and urbanisation. Value system, which was earlier favourable to the elderly has also experienced change under the influence of modernisation. Values like inter-dependence, co-operation and self-sacrifice are giving way to independence, personal mobility and personal achievement. All these factors have contributed to changes in the structure and functioning of the family system. As a consequence, the status and roles of the elderly have been severely affected. For instance, with introduction of television and computers, the story-telling function of grandmothers has become redundant. The grandchildren, often do not have time to share with their grandmothers. Doctors have replaced the midwifery and curing arts of the aged ladies. Now-a-days, food preservation is not required as already packaged vegetables and other edibles are easily available in the market. All these factors, have, undoubtedly snatched away important roles from the elderly women. This has resulted in corresponding reduction in the status. The role-less status has, indeed, increased dependence on others as well as vulnerability among the aged ladies. In view of these social, economic and technological changes, the contribution of the elderly women in the family has gone down, so is the case with their importance and acceptance in the family.

It may be pointed out that religion also acts as an instrument of social control, which in turn, ensured support and care for the elderly. It prescribes that, as it is the duty of parents to care for their offspring, in old age growing children have to serve their aged parents. It places caring for parents as '*dharma*' or duty of children and good will of old parents would bring prosperity in the family. Thus, cultural, social and religious imperatives enjoin upon the younger members to look after their elderly relatives. But, have these institutions been able to ensure well-being of the elderly?

Situation of the Elderly

The above discussion brings out that in the changing times, role and status of elderly women in the family and community have changed considerably, which has added their vulnerability. In this context, poverty, widowhood, migration of youngsters tend to put elderly women at risk of neglect and destitution. On the other hand, factors like support of the family and community play an important role in preventing marginalisation of the elderly women. Let us examine the roles of these factors in the present context.

The Researchers' Observation

Along with the interview schedule for the elderly women, a small observation sheet also formed the part of data collection tool. The first item of the observation sheet is appearance of the elderly respondent.

Information gathered shows that three per cent respondents look younger than their age, 54 per cent normal or in conformity with their age and the rest 43 per cent appear older than their age. In the context of vulnerability, the last category of 43 per cent respondents may be more marginalised.

Next, dress of the elderly women — whether fresh/used or mended — gives an indication of their well-being. Mended or frayed clothes do reflect social vulnerability. In this regard, 18 per cent respondents in the study were having mended/torn clothes, 13 per cent were in fresh clothes and 69 per cent women in used clothes.

Further, living or sleeping arrangements of elderly women have also been observed. Living in exclusive room would be an indicator of status and respect in the family while confinemint to *barsati* would reflect vulnerability of the aged women. In the study, 41 per cent respondents were observed to have exclusive room for them, 42 have to share their room with some family member and 17 per cent have only a *barsati* to live in.

Posture of family members towards elderly respondents certainly indicates the extent of vulnerability. Data show that in the case of 64 per cent elderly women, their family members were seen to be affectionate with them, 30 per cent were indifferent. Added to this, six per cent elderly women received disdainful treatment from their family members.

Daily Routine

Engagement in productive work, interactions with family and neighbourhood are considered to ensure status and respect for elderly women in the family. On the other hand, those who do not help in household chores, or do not have interactions with neighbours are believed to have problems in eliciting support when needed.

In the present study, elderly women were asked how much time they spent in doing household chores the previous day. There are 57 per cent elderly women who spend more than an hour attending household chores.

There are seven per cent respondents who have spent less than an hour. However, 36 per cent of elderly women do not spend any time in domestic activities. Would this speak well of their social adjustment?

Similarly, question was asked on time spent in community interactions. There are three-fourths of women (75 per cent) who do not interact with community people. Another three per cent elderly respondents spend less than an hour and 22 per cent more than an hour a day in interacting with the community. It would be readily seen that their interaction with community is but limited. Among other things, it is likely to add to their vulnerability.

Likewise, elderly women have been asked about the time they had spent in income-generating activities the previous day. In this regard, 77 per cent respondents had not spent any time in income-generating activities, merely one per cent had spent less than an hour and 22 per cent had spent more than an hour on income-generating activities.

It may be assumed that elderly women spending time in household chores, interaction with community people and in income-generating activities have acceptance and support of others which can go a long way in reducing vulnerability.

Elderly and Family

It goes without saying that, family plays a very important role in our life. It provides security, love, care, support and protection. In fact, in India, institutionalised care for the elderly is not popular as family is considered to be the primary support for the elderly. However, family, as an institution, is also, at times, a source of abuse and exploitation. Though lack of family support or having incongruent relationship with family members may put an elderly woman into a state of destitution.

This also paves the way for social vulnerability. Let us closely look into the role of family in reducing vulnerable conditions for elderly women.

Sleeping Place

Shelter or accommodation of the elderly in the household is a potential indicator of social vulnerability. It may be pointed out that this has become a problem of consequence particularly in view of urbanisation. It is observed that there are 45 per cent of elderly ladies who have a room exclusively for themselves, 36 per cent share sleeping arrangement with others and 15 per cent have to make do with a *barsati* or balcony. Are there any rural urban differences? Results bring out that there is a marginal difference in the rural-urban scene in sleeping place of respondents. Though urban environment is known for limited space, there is no difference of urban-rural setting, in terms of exclusive room meant for elderly ladies in 45 per cent cases. Share room is with 16 per cent women in rural areas and 13 per cent with their urban counterparts. Proportion of those in sharing room is slightly more in urban areas than those in rural areas, maybe because of space constraints usually in urban centers. There are more elderly women in rural areas (16 per cent) who have to resort to *barsati* or balcony than those in urban areas (13 per cent). Women sleeping in *barsati* may be treated as socially vulnerable and rural women have greater proportion in this category. Rest of the four per cent elderly women sleep in courtyard, backyard, outside house, etc. This indicates that nearly 19 per cent respondents may be socially vulnerable.

Have sleeping arrangement something to do with (total family) income? Diagram 6.1 presents relevant information. It is seen that elderly make-doing with balcony or barsati is proportionally less in medium and high-income groups. However, exclusive room for the elderly in the category of very low income attracts attention. Perhaps, these elderly mostly hail from rural areas.

Diagram 6.1

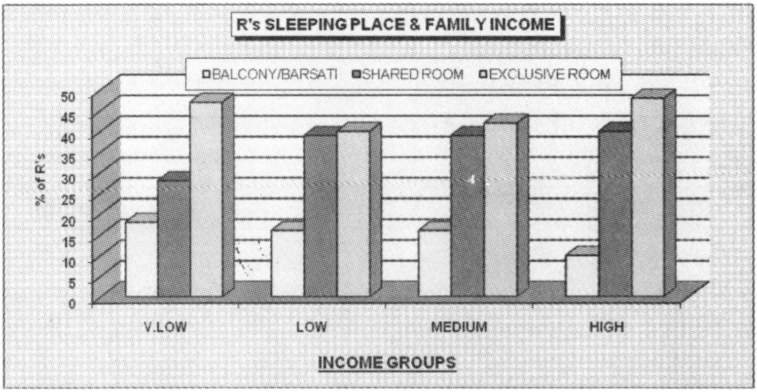

Handling of Household Chores

Involvement in household activities shows that elderly women have meaningful roles to perform; they are needed and accepted in the family. Contrarily, elderly women who are not involved in household activities often run the risk of being neglected or marginalised. However, involvement of elderly ladies in household chores has two opposite perspectives — if elderly women do household activities, it contributes towards their acceptance in the family. On the other hand, when aged women are impelled or compelled to do household chores, it becomes abuse. Let us see the situation in the present study.

Table 6.1 shows that most of the elderly women are involved in household activities willingly, with their own choice. Only a few women are forced to do the household chores. When seen in the context of involvement in household work, most of the elderly women are well accepted and do not run the risk of being neglected and marginalised.

Indeed, participation in household work is likely to differ in terms of age of the respondents. Data show that 63 per cent of elderly women, who are in the younger age group (60-64 years), spend more than an hour a-day on household chores. This proportion goes down to 57 per cent for those who are old (65-74 years) and still lower to 40 per cent in the case of old-old age group of 75 plus years.

Table 6.1: Activities Done by Respondents at Home (Percentage)

Daily Life Activities	*NO*	*Yes My Own choice*	*Yes Forced Upon Me*	*Total*
Preparing Tea/Coffee	47	52	2	100
Cutting Vegetables	27	71	2	100
Arranging Thing in Place	29	70	1	100
Cleaning Food Grains	44	52	4	100
Mending Clothes	59	39	2	100
Preparing Meals	45	51	4	100
Cleaning Utensils	45	52	2	100
Cleaning the Floors	37	60	3	100
Washing Clothes	44	52	5	100
Taking Care of Children	40	59	1	100
Involvement Income Generation	69	28	3	100

Diagram 6.2: R's (Daily) Participation in Household Chores.

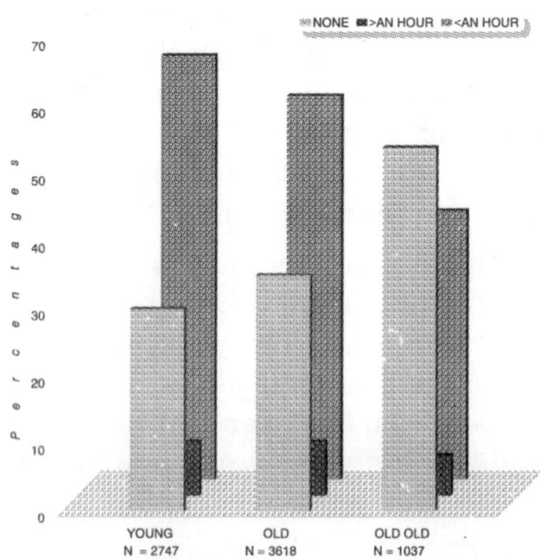

Widowhood

As argued earlier, marital status of a woman is considered to be a basis for her identity, security, worth and well-being. Widowhood, thus, becomes a major limiting condition. Earlier on there would be many sanctions imposed on widows, especially their involvement in religious ceremonies, social gatherings, and the like. They were expected to lead the simplest lifestyle duly reflected in their clothing, food and appearance.

In fact, widows were not supposed to have any interests or desire to pursue (Manjulata, 2003). Prakash (1994) reports that 'widowhood' weakens the kinship network from the husband's side and also loss of wife's role restricts certain social interactions. Do these restrictions on lifestyle and interactions still persist? Does widowhood bring loss of status and respect in the family and community? Let us see the situation in the present study.

Table 6.2: Change in Behaviour after Widowhood (Percentages)

Behaviour	*Yes*	*No*
Respect gone down	42	58
Neglect increased	43	57
Food clothing needs unmet	40	60
Medical care gone down	45	55
Community participation gone down	40	60
Shouting at R increased	24	76
Pushing R increased	19	81
Slapping/beating increased	20	80

In the study, widow respondents have been asked about the change in behaviour of family members and community people toward them after widowhood. Table 6.2 provides necessary details. There are a large proportion of elderly widows, who report that after widowhood, the respect and regard that they used to have in the family has decreased. Thus, we see that a little less than a-half of elderly widows have experienced emotional abuse after widowhood. Similarly, more than 40 per cent have experienced delay or postponement in meeting basic needs like food, clothing, medicare, etc. In the study, almost one-fourth face verbal abuse and nearly one in every five has experienced physical abuse, including slapping, beating, pushing, etc. Thus, widowhood, indeed, accentuate vulnerability among many elderly women.

Diagram 6.3

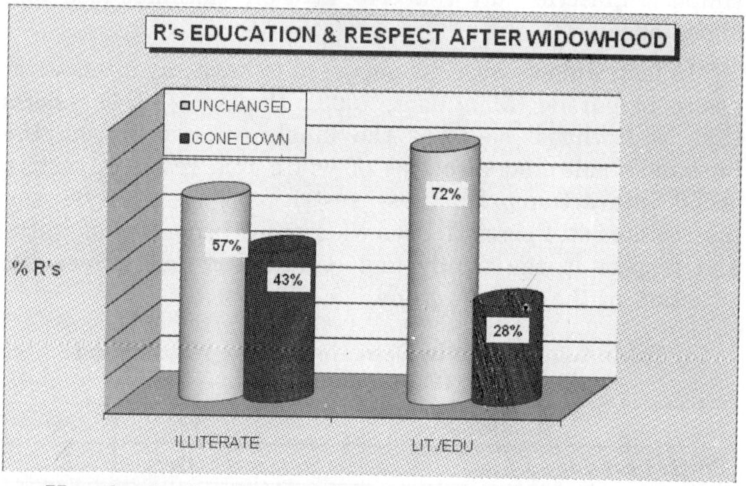

Has the decline in the status and respect have anything to do with the educational status of the widows? For this, the respondents are divided into two big groups, illiterate (N=6881) and literate or educated (N=544) Diagram 6.03 represents the situation as reported by the elderly widows. It would be readily seen that literate or educated widows are patently better off in this regard.

Below is the case study of a widow respondent who faced change in behaviour of her family after the demise of her husband.

Case History 6.1

> Durpada Adhikari, aged 81, is a Hindu widow living alone in a village in Sikkim. She lives in her mother's house, and her basic needs looked after by her younger brother.

> Durpada had once seen good days. She had 14 brothers and sisters and she was the oldest. In those days, girls used to be married young. She too, was married when she was 11 to a boy of 13. The boy came from a well-to-do family. They had no worries and were leading a blissful life. But all of a sudden their life changed. Her husband died at the young age of 28.
>
> Misery does not come alone. Since they had no issues, they had adopted a girl and had showered all their love and affection upon her. But after the death of her foster father, the adopted daughter turned wily. She grasped valuables and never returned.

Let us now look at the rural urban differentiation with regard to treatment with the elderly widow respondents. Data bring out marginal differences in community participation among widows in rural and urban areas – there are 39 per cent elderly widows in urban areas as compared to 40 per cent in rural ones who claim that after widowhood, their community participation has gone down. In the case of slackning of medical care, 43 per cent urban elderly widows were affirmative as compared to 45 per cent of their rural sisters. Similarly, 21 per cent of rural and 17 per cent, urban elderly widows report of physical abuse in terms of pushing and slapping, and beating going up after losing their spouse to death. This infers that rural elderly women are somewhat more vulnerable to physical abuse.

Added to this, in rural areas, the proportion of widows experiencing emotional abuse is slightly more than their urban counterparts. The basic needs of the elderly widows like food, clothing, medicare, in rural areas are more often ignored and postponed. There are 40 per cent aged widows in rural areas, as compared to 39 per cent of those in urban areas, facing decline in prompt fulfillment of their basic needs. However, in urban areas, elderly widows (43 per cent) are more frequently experiencing decline in regard and respect after widowhood than their rural sisters (41 per cent).

Table 6.3: Widowhood- General Neglect and Shouting at Respondent (Percentages)

Responses	*General Neglect*			*Shouting at R's*		
	Rural	*Urban*	*Total*	*Rural*	*Urban*	*Total*
Unchanged	57	58	57	75	78	76
Gone Down	43	42	43	25	22	24
Total	**100**	**100**	**100**	**100**	**100**	**100**

Likewise, Table 6.3 shows that in rural area general neglect against elderly widows are marginally more than that in urban areas. It is quite surprising when seen in the context of the popular belief that rural societies are more closed, traditional and abiding to moral and social ethos.

Elderly Abuse

Elderly abuse in the family is harassment or injustice, which is committed or which occurs in the domestic situation or perceived to be committed by their own family members (Kapur, 1996). Since it takes place within the four walls of the house it is very difficult to tackle. Statistical data in this regard are difficult to collect as in most of the cases it is seldom reported or reported differently. The abuse can be verbal, physical, psychological or emotional. It may include depriving the elderly of love, care, understanding and concern or neglecting their basic needs like food, clothing and medicare. In a few cases, the elderly may be thrown out of the house. Abandonment is a serious abuse that pushes an elderly to the verge of complete destitution, particularly, if she lacks economic resources to fall back upon.

Case History 6.2

Indrani, 90, has never been to school. She lives alone in a kutcha house in a village in Umaria district of Madhya Pradesh. She is a widow and neglected completely by her progeny sons. She has two grown-up sons. They live separately with their families and do not take care of her. Her clothes and bedding are invariably grimy. She remains unwell. In a half kutcha and half thatched house, lives the entire family. She sleeps in the thatched part of the house.

Indirani's family does not have any property. Her two sons and their wives work on farms for daily-wages. But, they do not get work all the days of a month. Poverty has engulfed the entire family. Though she has many serious health complaints, she finds it difficult to walk because of her age. The neighbours give her food from time to time and sometimes she has nothing to eat the whole day.

Often she goes to the nearby Anganwadi center, where she gets a little *dalia*. The Panchayat Sarpanch is quite sympathetic to her. He is trying to get her Old-Age Pension. In the mean time, he takes care of her clothing and bedding. There is a PHC also in the village. She gets medicine from it when needed.

The study brings out that a significant proportion of elderly women (11 per cent each) in rural and urban areas are experiencing verbal abuse. Manifestations of elderly abuse are many. It would be important to look into the rude behaviour or harsh treatment meted out to the elderly women. Diagram 6.04 brings out relevant details. Nearly 58 per cent of the elderly have been ignored or neglected, followed by about 19 per cent who have been shouted at or verbally abused.

Diagram 6.4

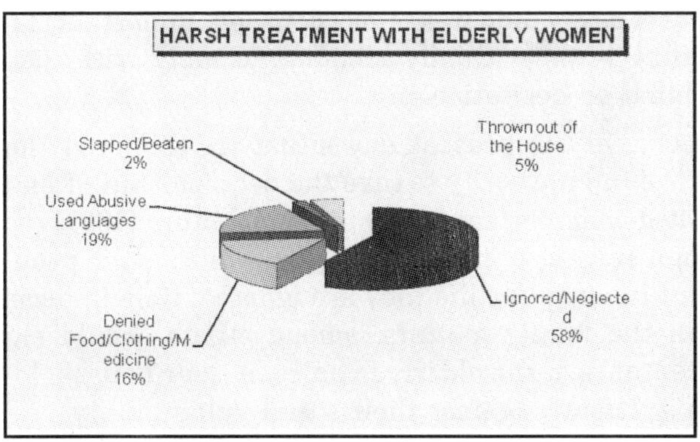

Table 6.4 shows that among the respondents facing abuse, majority have undergone emotional abuse, that is, being ignored and neglected. A significant proportion and more so in rural areas are denied their basic needs like food, clothing and medicare. Proportion of respondents experiencing verbal abuse is more in urban areas, while physical abuse and desertion is relatively common in rural areas. Data show a significant proportion of elderly being abused emotionally, verbally, physically. Definitely, it shows the gravity of their social vulnerability.

Table 6.4: Harsh Treatment of Elderly Women by Family Members (Percentages)

Responses	*Harshly Treatment*		
	Rural	*Urban*	*Total*
Ignored/Neglected	55	63	57
Denied Food, Clothing, Medicine etc.	18	13	16
Used Abusive Language	17	22	19
Slapped/Beaten/Thrashed	3	1	2
Thrown Out of the House	7	2	5
Total	**100**	**100**	**100**

Participation in Decision-making

It may be restated that in agrarian societies, the aged would, more often than not, play the role of the head of the household. They would take decisions on important family matters that younger family members comply with, usually without hitch or hesitation.

However, in the present day situation, the aged though have not the full authority to take the decisions but often they are consulted on important family matters. Luthra (1991) reports that though respect is ritualistically shown to older people in rituals, but in everyday life they are ignored. Role in decision-making in the family matters, among others, would signify social acceptance of the elderly females in their household and would be a defence against their social vulnerability.

Table 6.5: Elderly Women Consulted in Family Affairs (Percentages)

Consultant Matters	*Yes, Consult*
Gifts to Relatives	63
Buying Assets	58
Sale/Purchase of Property	57
Preparation of Daily Food Items	67
Marriage of Grand Children	67

In the study, the respondents have been asked about various issues on which family consults them while taking decision.

These issues range from giving gifts to relatives and friends to marriage of grandchildren. Table 6.5 shows the details. It brings out that women are more often consulted in the preparation of daily food items and marriage of grandchildren. Buying assets and sale/purchase of property requires knowledge about current market trends, about which, most often, elderly women do not have information. On the whole, majority of elderly women appear to be involved in decision-making process in their respective family groups.

Respect by Family Members

Giving respect to elderly is a social norm in Indian society. However, as discussed earlier, forces of change have challenged the ascribed status of senior citizens. Level of respect shown to the elderly women by their family members appears to have a direct relation with their social acceptance, and in turn, with their vulnerability. In the study, these women have been asked, "when the members of the family/household come from outside, do they do the following — come and wish you, sit and talk to you, consult you/share with you problems/ feelings".

Diagram 6.5 brings out the relevant details. It is observed that a majority of grown up sons and daughters etc. (58.3 per cent) do sit and talk with the elderly lady, when the comes from outside. Only 48.3 per cent of the sons and daughters are reported to ignore this custom. Let us take a close look at the possible differences between sons and daughters.

Diagram 6.5

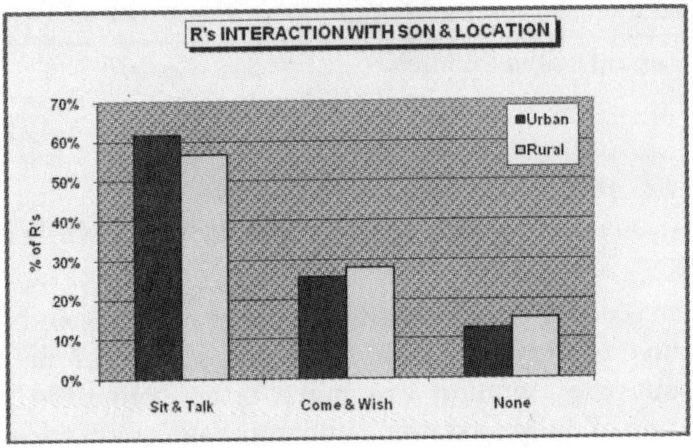

Table 6.6: Interaction with Son and Daughter (Percentages)

State	*Health Vulnerability*			
	Low	*Medium*	*High*	*Total*
Assam	18	44	38	100
Bihar	24	42	34	100
Chhattisgarh	44	26	30	100
Jharkhand	43	35	22	100
Madhya Pradesh	58	27	15	100
Orissa	45	34	21	100
Sikkim	51	33	16	100
Uttar Pradesh	23	37	40	100
Total	**38**	**35**	**27**	**100**

Table 6.6 gives the details of interaction with sons and daughters. In the context of vulnerability, respondents with whom their children do not interact are the most susceptible ones. Others sharing cordial relations with their offspring are less vulnerable. Data show that the proportion of respondents having no interaction with their sons in rural areas is marginally more than in the urban ones.

Table 6.12 brings out location-wise difference in interaction of elderly women with their sons-in-law and daughters-in-law. It shows that proportion of women whose sons-in-law and daughters-in-law do not interact with them is again more in rural areas and much higher than the proportion in the case of no-interaction with children. The case of Ram Bai emphasises the importance of cordial interactions with significant others.

Table 6.7: Interaction with Son-in-Law and Daughter-in-Law (Percentages)

Responses	*Son-In -Law*			*Daughter-In-Law*		
	Rural	*Urban*	*Total*	*Rural*	*Urban*	*Total*
Come and Wish	28	26	27	27	26	26
Sit & Talk	51	55	52	50	55	51
None	22	19	21	23	20	22
Total	**100**	**100**	**100**	**100**	**100**	**100**

Case History 6.3

Rambai, 70 is a widow. She lives with her married son and grandchildren in Madhya Pradesh. She has a happy and satisfied life with her family. Most of the day she sits in the verandah of her pucca house. She lost her husband about twelve years ago. She goes for morning walk daily to keep herself fit. She has cordial relations with all family members and takes initiative in doing domestic chores. She is involved in all the household decisions.

Rambai's daughter-in-law and sons take care of her well and shower their love and respect on her. She has one exclusive room for herself. Widowhood has hardly changed her status at all and the community and the family. Rambai's financial position is also healthy. The big house worth Rs. 8 lakh is in her name.

Table 6.8: Interaction with Husband and Grand-Children (Percentages)

Responses	*Husband*			*Grand-Children*		
	Rural	*Urban*	*Total*	*Rural*	*Urban*	*Total*
Come and Wish	13	13	13	30	31	30
Sit & Talk	54	54	54	54	57	55
None	33	32	33	16	12	15
Total	**100**	**100**	**100**	**100**	**100**	**100**

Table 6.8 gives details of elderly women's interaction with their husbands and grandchildren. Again, we observe a significant proportion of elderly women having differential relations with their husbands. In contrast, grandchildren appear to be more differential towards them.

Interaction with Neighbours

In a way neighbours represents the community in which one lives. Besides, they provide security, assistance, companionship and guidance. Physical proximity makes the neighbours a source of immediate help in case of any need. Blau (1961) reports that older people suffering critical role losses are most likely to have neighbours as friends who have encountered similar losses.

However, it is often claimed that cities, particularly metropolitan ones, have loosely defined neighbourhood and different community life. Fast pace of life in urban area does not leave any time for interaction between neighbours. Reportedly the situation in rural areas is relatively better. What is the situation in the study states?

Data bring out information on elderly womens' interactions with neighbours/friends, including sitting and talking with them. It is observed that only one elderly woman out of every eight has a steady interaction with neighbours. Out of varied modes of interactions with neighbours, data show that most common is shared morning walk followed by participation in religious discourses. A few more details in this regard could be appropriate. Added to this, there is marginal difference among illiterate and literate or educated elderly women and their level of interaction with neighbours. Quite surprisingly, unlike the popular belief, urban elderly women have more frequent interaction with their neighbours than their rural counterparts. Ninety per cent of urban and 87 per cent of rural elderly women are talking to their neighbours on regular basis. Likewise, 28 per cent rural and 29 per cent urban elderly women are going for morning/evening walks with their neighbours. Further, 57 per cent of elderly women are visiting places of worships and 34 per cent are attending discourses with their neighbours. There are no noticeable differences between rural and urban elderly women in their interaction pattern with their neighbours.

Community Involvement

Apart from family, community also plays an important role in ensuring social support, care and well-being of the elderly. In rural areas, traditionally, *panchayats* have been formal institutions representing community. This has been further reinforced following the 73rd amendment of the constitution. In a way, *sarpanchs* and other *panchas* make for elders in the community, they also act or react informally. Often they resolve familial and property-conflicts and take decisions regarding the welfare of the village.

Viewing the scenario from the gender perspective, women would remain in the four walls of the household and, in general, would have restricted interaction with the community people. May be this is not shown with *panchayat* members particularly women *panchayat* members. How is the interaction of elderly women with their community people?

Results show that 13 per cent elderly women have interactions with *panchayat* leaders. Most of them do not interact with elected leaders and among those who interact, proportion of rural elderly women is slightly larger than their urban counterparts.

Further, details of membership of respondents in such organisations as self-help group, mahila mandal, gram panchayat, etc., present dismal picture - there is only one per cent proportion of elderly women having membership of Mahila

Mandals, one per cent of self-help groups and one per cent of gram panchayat. There are no elderly women in gram panchayats in Assam, Bihar, Jharkhand and Uttar Pradesh. On the other hand, SHGs seem to be somewhat popular. Except Uttar Pradesh, all states record membership of elderly women, though, merely one to three per cent. Mahila Mandals are, in comparison, popular as at least one per cent of elderly women are part of these groups in all the study states. It is often held that association of women with any formal groups like self help groups, mahila mandals, panchayat, etc., provides social support which, in turn, acts as bulwork against dependence and vulnerability. In that context, most of the elderly respondents may be socially vulnerable as compared with their male counterparts. However, the findings are in consonance with the popular belief that formal and informal interactions of women with the community have been woefully small, recent constitutional changes notwithstanding.

The present section underlines those dimensions, which limit or accelerate social vulnerability among elderly women. Many among them appear to have discordant relationship with family members, manifestations of which may be observed through unwilling participation in household chores, elderly abuse, discrimination on being widow and the like. Lack of interaction with neighbours and community people also tend to increase social vulnerability among them. The section, which follows, would among other things deal with a few other pertinent dimensions of social vulnerability.

7

Vulnerability: Risk Factors

Existentially everybody is vulnerable, the elderly, particularly elderly women are more so vulnerable. Of late, the elderly have emerged as a prominent vulnerable group in ways more than one. In the case of elderly women, vulnerability is accentuated manifolds due to certain peculiar health conditions as well as social factors emanating from the within the patriarchal social context. On the other hand, elderly women are gradually but surely, outnumbering their male counterparts in most countries. This trend is global, though at a varying rate. Therefore, we observe that ageing is an increasing experience of females.

Vulnerability, in its simplest denotative sense, means the capacity to be harmed. It is the potential for negative outcomes or consequences. However, although most scholars agree on this broad definition, the use of the term varies depending upon the discipline and research issue. Cutter (1996) identifies three distinct clusters of definitions for vulnerability: as risk of exposure to hazards, as a capability for social response (what we call below coping or adaptive capacity), and as an attribute of places (e.g., vulnerability of coastlines to sea level rise).

For the present study, vulnerability is taken to be as the condition or state of some persons or groups who somehow carry a larger probability of being harmed by economic, environmental or health or social problems, than the rest of the population. Vulnerability is taken to be the contingent conditions that hamper the well-being (social functioning) of the elderly women and require a support system in addition to the existing ones to mitigate the factors that threaten their well being, if not encountered promptly.

Vulnerability among the elderly is a complex phenomenon. It is more complex in the context of the elderly women. Nonetheless, the quest for a deeper understanding must go on. This is what has been attempted in the present study. Towards this, a few observable and dependable items, have been identified and incorporated in the main tool of data collection, namely, interview schedule that has been canvassed on the elderly women in different states of the country. Let us take a close look:

Economic Vulnerability

As discussed in Chapter Five, many conditions accentuate economic vulnerability of the elderly women. In order to facilitate further analysis, a composite variable, namely economic vulnerability, has been developed combining the following items/variables. Following scalogram technique (also see www.socialresearchmethods.net) those responses have been recoded in accordance with the weightage indicated below:

HQ 3.12 Are there any items of expenditure (house renovation, child's marriage, *teerth yatra, ham*, etc., which are held up for want of money?

1 Yes	(Weightage)	2
2 No		1
9 NA / DK / NR		1

Q. 3.13 Can you easily spend money for buying such items of necessity as clothes, eatables, etc.?

1 Yes	(Weightage)	1
2 No		2
9 NA / DK / NR		2

Q. 3.14 Are you able to spend money on making '*daan*' or donations to temple, church or other religious institutions as per your wishes?

1 Yes	(Weightage)	1
2 No		2
9 NA / DK / NR		2

Q. 3.15 If ever you need some expensive medical treatment for yourself, do you think you can arrange money for it?

1 Yes (Weightage)	1
2 No	2
9 NA / DK / NR	2

Q. 3.16 Do your family members willingly meet your routine expenses?

1 Yes (Weightage)	1
2 No	2
9 NA / DK / NR	2

Q. 9.4 (Caregiver) Are the expenses on this elderly lady a burden on the family budget?

1 No (Weightage)	1
2 Yes	2
9 NA / DK / NR	1

Subsequently, the values of the above-mentioned six items have been recoded and summated to have scores and a new composite variable has been generated. It has theoretical score as well as observed score, which ranges from 6 and 12. Utilising these scores, yet another variable, with grouped scores, has been computed. It has three categories: Low (score, 6-8), Medium (9-10), and High (11-12).

Results show that there are 27 per cent elderly women in the low category (27 per cent in rural and 28 per cent in urban areas), 50 per cent in medium (49 per cent in rural and 51 per cent in urban areas) and 23 per cent in high economic vulnerability (24 per cent in rural and 21 per cent in urban areas). Location-wise analysis of economic vulnerability among the elderly women shows that there are marginal differences in the level of economic vulnerability among the rural and urban the elderly women, with more women having high economic vulnerability in rural areas.

Diagram 7.1 presents age-wise economic vulnerability among the elderly women. About a half of the elderly women in all the age groups have medium vulnerability. Data analysis show that economic vulnerability tends to increase with age.

Diagram 7.1

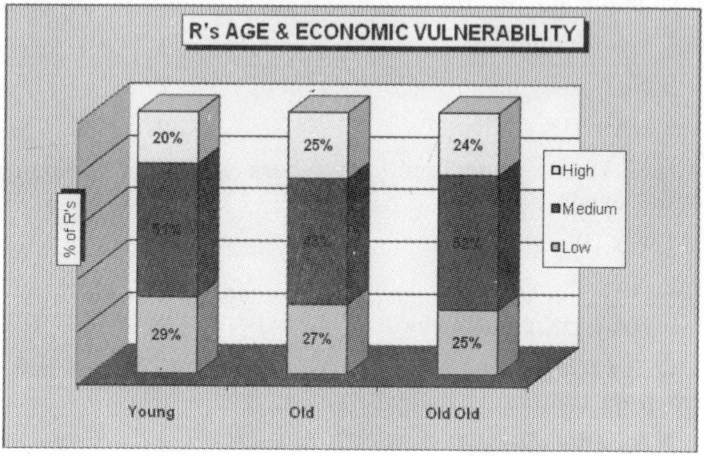

Table 7.1: Economic vulnerability and the state Elderly women belong to (Percentages)

State	*Economic Vulnerability*			
	Low	*Medium*	*High*	*Total*
Assam	24	70	6	100
Bihar	11	48	41	100
Chhattisgarh	24	37	39	100
Jharkhand	40	47	13	100
Madhya Pradesh	42	38	20	100
Orissa	17	62	21	100
Sikkim	45	49	6	100
Uttar Pradesh	17	46	37	100
Total	**27**	**50**	**23**	**100**

Table 7.1 shows that Sikkim, Madhya Pradesh and Jharkhand have maximum proportions of respondents with low-economic vulnerability. In the category of medium-economic vulnerability, Assam, Orissa and Bihar dominate. Highest proportions of women with high-economic vulnerability are in Bihar, Chhattisgarh and Uttar Pradesh. This trend also confirms to other economic indicators of these states.

Health Vulnerability

Another composite variable, 'Health Vulnerability', has been developed to have a holistic view. Health vulnerability is taken, which comprises (a) Nutritional vulnerability, (b) Sensory vulnerability, (c) Physical vulnerability, (d) Mental health vulnerability, and (e) ADL (Activities of Daily Life) vulnerability. Details are as follows —

(a) Nutritional Vulnerability

Q. 4.3a What did you have in your meals yesterday? Cereals (chapatti / rice, etc.)

1 Did not have (Weightage)	2
2 Had adequately	1
3 Somewhat inadequate	2
4 Inadequate	3
9 NA / DK / NR	2

Q. 4.3b What did you have in your meals yesterday? Pulses

1 Did not have (Weightage)	2
2 Had adequately	1
3 Somewhat inadequate	2
4 Inadequate	3
9 NA / DK / NR	2

Q. 4.3c What did you have in your meals yesterday? Eggs/ poultry / meat

1 Did not have (Weightage)	2
2 Had adequately	1
3 Somewhat inadequate	2
4 Inadequate	3
9 NA / DK / NR	2

Q. 4.3d What did you have in your meals yesterday? Milk/ milk products

1 Did not have (Weightage)	2
2 Had adequately	1
3 Somewhat inadequate	2

4 Inadequate	3
9 NA / DK / NR	2

Q. 4.3e What did you have in your meals yesterday? Green vegetables / salads

1 Did not have (Weightage)	2
2 Had adequately	1
3 Somewhat inadequate	2
4 Inadequate	3
9 NA / DK / NR	2

Q. 4.3f What did you have in your meals yesterday? Fruits

1 Did not have (Weightage)	2
2 Had adequately	1
3 Somewhat inadequate	2
4 Inadequate	3
9 NA / DK / NR	2

Weighted in the values above-mentioned six items have been summated, adopting the Scalogram (Guttman) Technique. A fresh composite variable has been generated. It has theoretical scores 6 to18 (observed score, 6-15). Utilising these scores, yet another variable, with grouped scores, has been computed. It has three categories: Low (6-9), Medium (10-11), and High (12-15).

(b) 'Sensory' Vulnerability

Q. 4.4a During the last five years, what has been the position of vision?

1 Improved (Weightage)	1
2 Unchanged	2
3 Gone down	3
9 NA / DK / NR	2

Q. 4.4b During last five years, what has been the position of bones / joints?

1 Improved (Weightage)	1
2 Unchanged	2

3 Gone down 3

9 NA / DK / NR 2

Q. 4.4c During the last five years, what has been the position of hearing?

1 Improved (Weightage) 1

2 Unchanged 2

3 Gone down 3

9 NA / DK / NR 2

Q. 4.4d During the last five years, what has been the position of psychomotor/trembling?

1 Improved (Weightage) 1

2 Unchanged 2

3 Gone down 3

9 NA / DK / NR 2

The values of the above above-mentioned four items have been indexed, to have scores, and a new composite variable has been generated. Its theoretical and observed score ranges between 4 and 12. Utilising these scores, yet another variable, with grouped scores, has been computed. It has three categories: Low (4-9), Medium (10-11), and High (score, 12).

(c) Physical Vulnerability

Q. 4.5a During the last one year, have you had any medical complaints — Blood pressure?

1 Yes (Weightage) 2

2 No 1

9 NA / DK / NR 1

Q. 4.5b During the last one year, have you had any medical complaints — Heart problem?

1 Yes (Weightage) 2

2 No 1

9 NA / DK / NR 1

Q. 4.5c During the last one year, have you had any medical complaints — gynecological problem?

1 Yes (Weightage) 2

2 No 1

9 NA / DK / NR 1

Q. 4.5d During the last one year, have you had any medical complaints — sugar/diabetes?

1 Yes (Weightage) 2

2 No 1

9 NA / DK / NR 1

Q. 4.5e During the last one year, have you had any medical complaints — digestive upsets?

1 Yes (Weightage) 2

2 No 1

9 NA / DK / NR 1

Q. 4.5f During the last one year, have you had any medical complaints — coughing?

1 Yes (Weightage) 2

2 No 1

9 NA / DK / NR 1

Q. 4.5g During the last one year, have you had any medical complaints — stones?

1 Yes (Weightage) 2

2 No 1

9 NA / DK / NR 1

Q. 4.5h During the last one year, have you had any medical complaints — jaundice?

1 Yes (Weightage) 2

2 No 1

9 NA / DK / NR 1

The values of these eight items have been summated, and a new composite variable has been generated. Its theoretical and observed score is between 8 to 16. Observed scores have been grouped and a new variable has been computed. It has three categories: Low (score, 8), Medium (score, 9), and High (10-16).

(d) Mental Health Vulnerability

Q. 4.6a During the last one year, have you had any complaints — anxiety and tension?

1 Yes (Weightage)	2
2 No	1
9 NA / DK / NR	1

Q. 4.6b During the last one year, have you had any complaints — sleeplessness/insomnia?

1 Yes (Weightage)	2
2 No	1
9 NA / DK / NR	1

Q. 4.6c During the last one year, have you had any complaints of mental pressure/depression?

1 Yes (Weightage)	2
2 No	1
9 NA / DK / NR	1

Adhering to the scaling technique, the values of these three items have been summated, and a new composite variable has been developed. Its theoretical and observed score is between 3 and 6. These scores have been categorised and a new variable has been generated. It has three groups: Low (score, 3), Medium (score, 4), and High (5-6).

(e) ADL Vulnerability

We would like to have some information about your daily life activities.

Q. 4.17a Can you do 'eating'?

1 On my own (Weightage)	1
2 Require help	2
9 NA / DK / NR	1

Q. 4.17b Can you do 'bathing'?

1 On my own (Weightage)	1
2 Require help	2
9 NA / DK / NR	1

Q. 4.17c Can you do 'walking'?

1 On my own (Weightage)	1
2 Require help	2
9 NA / DK / NR	1

Q. 4.17d Can you do 'getting up'?

1 On my own (Weightage)	1
2 Require help	2
9 NA / DK / NR	1

Q. 4.17e Can you do 'kitchen work'?

1 On my own (Weightage)	1
2 Require help	2
9 NA / DK / NR	1

Q. 4.17f Can you do 'taking medicine'?

1 On my own (Weightage)	1
2 Require help	2
9 NA / DK / NR	1

Q. 4.17g Can you do 'washing'?

1 On my own (Weightage)	1
2 Require help	2
9 NA / DK / NR	1

The values obtained from the responses of these seven items have been summated, and a new composite variable has been generated. Its theoretical and observed score is between 7 and 14. In turn, these scores have been grouped and a new variable has been computed. It has three categories: Low (score, 7), Medium (8-9), and High (10-14).

Health (overall) Vulnerability

Let us restate: Health vulnerability is assumed to have five components:

(a) Nutritional vulnerability

1 Low (Weightage)	1
2 Medium	2
3 High	3

(b) 'Sensory' vulnerability

1 Low (Weightage)	1
2 Medium	2
3 High	3

(c) Physical vulnerability

1 Low (Weightage)	1
2 Medium	2
3 High	3

(d) Mental health vulnerability

1 Low (Weightage)	1
2 Medium	2
3 High	3

(e) ADL vulnerability

1 Low (Weightage)	1
2 Medium	2
3 High	3

The weighted values of these five items have been summated, and new composite variable health (overall) vulnerability has been generated. Its theoretical and observed score is between 5 and 15. Next, these scores have been grouped and a new variable has been computed. It has three groups: Low (5-8), Medium (9-10), and High (11-15). It is these variables, which has been subjected to a detailed analysis. Results show that 38 per cent elderly women have low health vulnerability, 35 per cent medium and 27 per cent high health vulnerability. It shows that most of them have low or medium vulnerability.

Diagram 7.2 brings out age-wise health vulnerability among elderly women. It clearly shows that with advancing age health vulnerability tends to increase. In the category of high vulnerability, proportion of old-old elderly women is almost double their young counterparts.

Q. 5.3h Now, please tell us the activities you generally do at home:

Cleaning/sweeping the floor:

1 No (Weightage)	2
2 Yes, by choice	1
3 Yes, forced upon me	3
9 NA / DK / NR	2

Q. 5.3i Now, please tell us the activities you generally do at home:

Washing clothes / laundering:

1 No (Weightage)	2
2 Yes, by choice	1
3 Yes, forced upon me	3
9 NA / DK / NR	2

Q. 5.3j Now, please tell us the activities you generally do at home:

Taking care of children:

1 No (Weightage)	2
2 Yes, by choice	1
3 Yes, forced upon me	3
9 NA / DK / NR	2

Q. 5.3k Now, please tell us the activities you generally do at home:

Involvement in income-generation:

1 No (Weightage)	2
2 Yes, by choice	1
3 Yes, forced upon me	3
9 NA / DK / NR	2

The responses of these eleven items have been summated, and a new composite variable has been developed. Its theoretical and observed score is between 11 and 33. In turn, the observed scores have been grouped and a new variable has been computed. It has three groups: Low (11-13), Medium (14-19), and High (20-33).

(c) Elderly abuse

Q. 5.6 Do any of the family members rudely behave with you?

1 Yes (Weightage)	2
2 No	1
9 NA / DK / NR	1

Q. 5.7 Quite a few elderly women are reportedly treated harshly in the household. During the last one year, has any member of the household done any of the following?

1 Ignored or neglected you (Weightage)	2
2 Denied food, clothing or medical care	2
3 Used abusive language with you	3
4 Slapped, beat or thrashed you	3
5 Thrown you out of the house	3
9 NA / DK / NR	1

The values of the above-noted two items have been summated, and a new composite variable has been generated. Its theoretical and observed score is between 2 and 5. In turn, the observed scores have been grouped and a new variable has been computed. It has three groups: Low (score, 2), Medium (score, 3), and High (4-5).

(d) Interviewer/researcher Observations

7.3 Living / sleeping arrangements —

1 Exclusive (Weightage)	1
2 Shared	2
3 *Barsati*	3
9 NA / DK / NR	2

7.4 Posture of family members towards R —

1 Affectionate (Weightage)	1
2 Indifferent	2
3 Disdainful	3
9 NA / DK / NR	2

Responses to the above two items have been assigned values and summated, and a new composite variable has been generated. Its theoretical and observed score is between 2 and 6. Next, these scores have been grouped and a new variable

Table 7.3 shows that Sikkim and Assam have the highest proportions of elderly women with low social vulnerability. Are these women well integrated with their social milieu? On the other hand, in the category of medium-social vulnerability, Orissa and Bihar figure dominantly. A highest proportion of elderly women with high-social vulnerability are in Uttar Pradesh and Bihar. It would be recorded that these states are also prominent in terms of economic vulnerability; it is that economic vulnerability also foster social vulnerability or visa-versa?

Overall Vulnerability

In order to measure overall vulnerability, a composite variable, combining economic vulnerability, health vulnerability and social vulnerability, and taking code categories as weights has been developed. The new variable has theoretical and observed range from 3 to 9. The observed score has been divided into three groups — Low (3-4), Medium (5-6) and High (7-9).

In the study, 49 per cent of aged women have low-overall vulnerability, 20 per cent have medium and 31 per cent have high-overall vulnerability. This shows that nearly one-third of the aged women are highly vulnerable while about a-half have low overall vulnerability.

Diagram 7.4

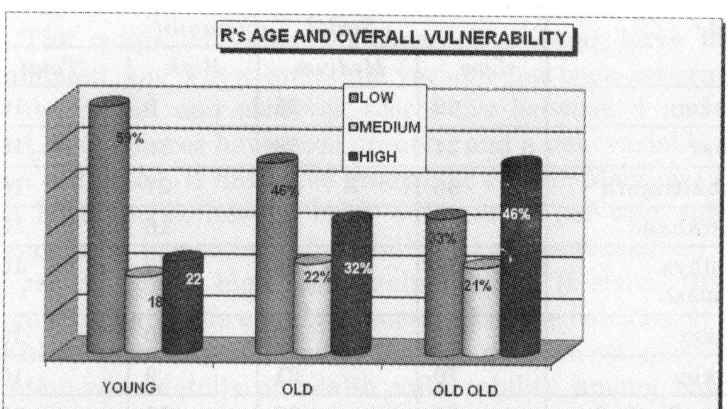

Diagram 7.4 shows age-wise overall vulnerability among the elderly women. It brings out that with advancing age

overall vulnerability tends to increase. In the category of high overall vulnerability, proportion of old-old elderly women is almost double of those in the young category.

Analysis of the location-wise details of overall vulnerability among the elderly women show marginal differences in the level of social vulnerability among the rural and urban elderly women – there are 30 per cent of aged women in rural areas with high overall vulnerability in contrast to 32 per cent of their counterparts in the urban areas. In the medium overall vulnerability category, there are 21 per cent aged women in rural areas and 19 per cent in urban setting. In both, rural and urban areas, 49 per cent (each) of the elderly women are ranked in the low-overall vulnerability category.

Table 7.4: Size of the Family of the Elderly Women and Overall Vulnerability (Percentages)

Size of family	*Low*	*Medium*	*High*	*Total*
Single	43	20	37	100
Small (2-4)	51	19	30	100
Medium (5-6)	49	21	30	100
Large (7-24	51	21	28	100

Overall vulnerability also been classified in terms of the size of the family of the elderly women (see Table 7.04). It would be seen that more than a-half of the elderly women are in the 'low category' and their proportion in the 'high category' is relatively small. In contrast, single women are proportionately more in the category of high vulnerability. Perhaps large household have a wider and stronger safety-net.

Table 7.5: Marital Status and Overall Vulnerability (Percentages)

Marital Status	*Low*	*Medium*	*High*	*Total*
Married	57	18	25	100
Widow/Unmarried	44	22	34	100
Total	**49**	**20**	**31**	**100**

8

Social Support Structure

Social support is a distinctive feature of human society. Directly and indirectly, family, community, state, provides much needed social support. On the other hand, the elderly need social support most. When their physical and mental energy have waned and they have no one to turn to, social institutions need to stand by them (Khan, 1997). This would provide them relief and instill, among others, a sense of social belongingness, a measure of confidence in the social structure.

In this regard, India has a long tradition. In ancient times, care of the elderly used to be the responsibility, successively, of the family, village and the king. Contemporary world, however, is somewhat different. Rapid and massive changes in social, political and economic spheres of life have considerably altered time-honoured traditions. This calls for the organisation or streamlining of substitutive services.

As discussed in the preceding chapters, there is much, which could be done by the family, community and the elderly themselves. Nevertheless, there are quite a few areas in which public assistance would be required. For instance, statistics have shown that about one-third of the elderly are living below poverty line and another one-third just above it (see NSSO, 1997). So, it is evident these two-thirds of older persons face economic hardship and require support for earning a livelihood. No doubt, something has been done in recent years in this regard. The present chapter attempts a stock-taking of services evolved for senior citizens and their accessibility, availability, reach and impact vis-à-vis the elderly in the study area.

status of migration was looked into as it directly influences the situation of the elderly. Young persons migrate to cities and industrial centres in search of work and opportunity. Often they take along their families, leaving behind their elderly parents to keep a watch on the house, cattle, etc.

Diagram 8.1

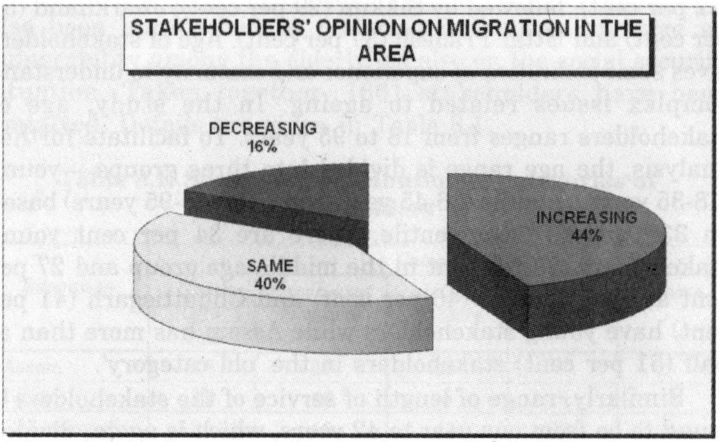

Diagram 8.1 brings out information on migration trends according to the lengths of stay of the stakeholders in the area. A majority of stakeholders report that migration is increasing, perhaps by the year. But there are some of them who feel that it is decreasing. May it be noted that this also includes those who have been in the area for long. Does this opinion differ in various states? State-wise details of migration in the study area show that Uttar Pradesh and Bihar are the source of maximum out-migration. Sikkim has maintained status quo in migration and in Chhattisgarh, it is reportedly decreasing.

The stakeholders have been asked about the existence of elderly-specific services in their area. How about Geriatric units in hospitals? In the study, 62 per cent of the stakeholders maintained that there are no geriatric units in their respective areas while 17 per cent said that there are some. Rest of the stakeholders were unsure of availability of geriatric units in their area. Larger number of stakeholders confirmed presence of geriatric units in Uttar Pradesh (36 per cent), followed by

Sikkim (30 per cent) and Chhattisgarh (27 per cent). Lowest proportions of stakeholders confirming presence of geriatric unit are in Jharkhand (one per cent), Madhya Pradesh (three per cent) and Assam (four per cent). In Orissa six per cent and in Bihar 12 per cent stakeholders confirm presence of geriatric units in their respective areas.

The stakeholders have further been asked to provide information on health-seeking behaviour of elderly women in their area. Where do they go when ailing? Data show that majority of the elderly go to government hospitals and almost one-fourth prefer private hospitals. Table 8.2 shows state-wise distribution of ailing elderly's health-seeking behaviour. In Sikkim and Orissa, a majority of the elderly prefer going to government hospitals. Jharkhand and Uttar Pradesh have private health settings, as more preferred ones by elderly women. In Chhattisgarh, Madhya Pradesh and Uttar Pradesh more than 10 per cent elderly opt for other health-seeking measures like resorting to home remedies, going to ojhas, quacks, etc.

Table 8.2: Stakeholders' view on elderly women's preference in availing health care facility (Percentages)

State	*Government Hospital*	*Private Hospital*	*Any Other*	*Total*
Assam	68	30	2	100
Bihar	57	34	9	100
Chattisgarh	67	18	15	100
Jharkhand	55	43	2	100
Madhya Pradesh	67	21	12	100
Orissa	81	10	9	100
Sikkim	91	5	3	100
Uttar Pradesh	46	43	11	100
Total	**66**	**26**	**8**	**100**

In ancient times, the elderly did enjoy respect from their younger generation. It also provided them a social safety net against vulnerability to abuse and destitution.The stakeholders have been asked to comment on the respect given by the younger generation to their elderly relatives. Diagram 8.2 shows that most of the stakeholders feel that respect and status has gone down. Indeed, this would be having repercussion on the well-being of the elderly. Maximum stakeholders from Madhya Pradesh feel that younger generation is less respectful to the elderly in the present times. More than one-third stakeholders from Sikkim feel that respect given to elderly is same as before while nearly one-third stakeholders from the same state feel that boys and girls are more respectful.

Diagram 8.2

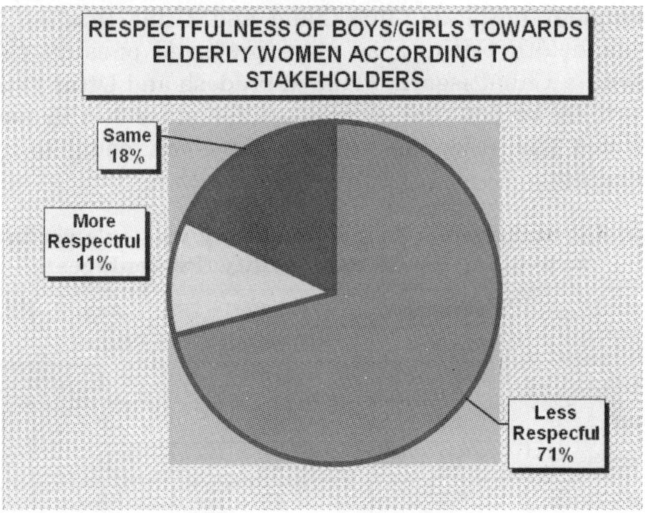

Let us, now, pay attention to state-wise details of stakeholders' view on cases being registered under section 125 of the Criminal Procedure Code. Data show that largest number of stakeholders reporting registration of cases under section 125 is largest in Uttar Pradesh (nine per cent) followed by Orissa (eight per cent) and Bihar (six per cent).

It may be noted that in a large number of cases of elderly abuse remain unreported (see Kapur, 1996). Reasons for this may be a lack of awareness or even inhibition to go against their offspring among the elderly women. This apart, enforcement of provision of the court of criminal procedure does not appear to be much vigorous.

Abuse against elderly has remained under the shadow of secrecy due to reasons more than one. Fear of social stigma is one of the salient reasons for non-reporting and under-reporting of cases of elderly abuse. Dependence on offspring, economically and emotionally, forces elderly women not to aggravate the situation and quietly tolerate abuse. In this regard, the stakeholders' view was taken on this, have they heard of cases of physical violence against elderly women? Maximum proportion is from Orissa (25 per cent) followed by Madhya Pradesh (20 per cent), Uttar Pradesh (18 per cent), Jharkhand (17 per cent), Chhattisgarh (13 per cent) and Bihar (eight per cent). Least proportion, two per cent, of stakeholders from Assam and Sikkim each affirmed cases of physical violence against elderly women.

In this connection, stakeholders' opinion about criminal cases against the elderly has been ascertained. A large number of stakeholders from Madhya Pradesh (22 per cent) report an increase in crime rate against the elderly. Uttar Pradesh comes next with 15 per cent. Interestingly, most of the stakeholders from Chhattisgarh (68 per cent) maintain that the crime rate is decreasing in their area. None of the stakeholders from Assam affirmed increasing crime rate against elderly. On an average, nine per cent stakeholders opined increase in crime rate and 64 per cent maintained decreasing crime against the elderly.

As part of social support system, existence of yoga clubs, *mahila mandals*, Self-Help Groups (SHGs) for elderly women in their community, help in reducing their vulnerability. Results present that little more than a-half of the stakeholders affirm presence of SHGs in their area. Among those who affirm the existence of SHGs, 70 per cent maintain that there are many women SHGs also. Very few stakeholders maintain presence of Yoga clubs in their area. Next, almost a half (49 per cent) of the stakeholders inform the existence of *mahila mandals*. Further, 32 per cent stakeholders are of the opinion that these *mahila mandals* are active, while the rest feel otherwise. Among these active *mahila mandals* only nine per cent are doing some activities for elderly women.

The stakeholders have further been asked whether NGOs, in their area, have received grants from Ministry of Social Justice and Empowerment for organising programmes and activities for the elderly. There are seven per cent stakeholders who affirm and rest of them deny. On further probing whether any NGOs have tried getting grants, only nine per cent stakeholders have respond in the affirmative.

The opinion of stakeholder has been ascertained about services and programmes for the elderly. Merely two per cent stakeholders have reported that counseling services or pre-retirement counseling is provided to the elderly in their area. Rest of the 98 per cent stakeholders have denied existence of such services. Further, 16.8 per cent stakeholders report that there is Legal Aid Cells (LAC). But only five per cent stakeholders confirm that there are some special arrangements for elderly in the LAC like free legal aid, etc. When asked about the number of beneficiaries, only 49 (three per cent) stakeholders have provided some information. The numbers of beneficiaries range from one to 22 only.

Programmes and Schemes

India is avowedly a democratic and welfare state. Given this, the government has responded to the social security needs of the elderly. In order to reduce the vulnerability of elderly persons, the state has intervened through various programmes and schemes, some of the significant ones, need to be highlighted and their reach indicated.

Diagram 8.3

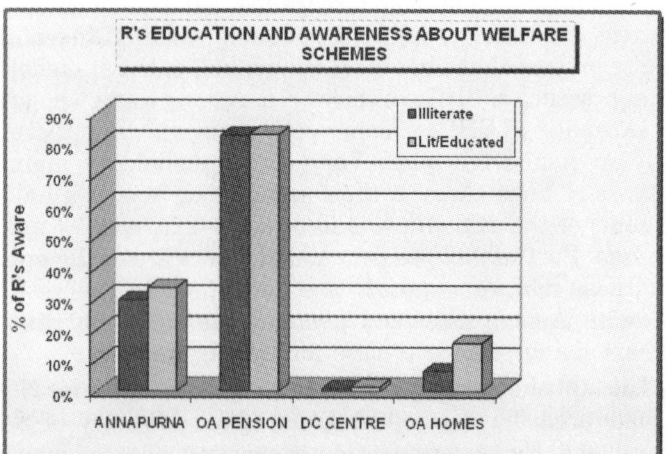

Diagram 8.3 attempts to provide and overview from the perspective of the elderly persons. It would be readily seen that both illiterate and literate elderly ladies are informed on old age pension schemes. However, information and awareness about Annapurna Scheme is moderate and so is in the case of Old Age Homes. Knowledge about Day Care Centers is abysmally low. Perhaps district information officers and district welfare officers need to pay attention in this regard. Next, various programmes and schemes need to be focalised.

Annapurna Scheme

The Ministry of Rural Development, GOI, launched this scheme on the 1st April 2000. The Annapurna scheme aims at providing food security by meeting the requirement of those Senior Citizens who are eligible but have remained uncovered by the National Old Age Pension Scheme (NOAPS). Implemented by Food, Civil Supplies and Consumer Protection Department, Annapurna Scheme provides 10 kilograms of food grains (rice or wheat or both) free of cost to the beneficiaries. There is, however, a ceiling on the total number of Annapurna beneficiaries. At least 20 per cent of the persons eligible to receive pension under NOAPS would have Annapurna to fall back upon. It is applicable to destitute elderly persons, both male and female. Senior persons aged 65 years or more, who are destitute (having no regular income of their own or who do not get support from family members) are eligible to avail this scheme.

At the state level, the Department of Public Distribution, Department of Food, Civil Supplies and Consumer Affairs, and at the district level, the Collector/District Magistrate/Chief Executive Officer, Zila Panchayat is responsible for the implementation of the Annapurna scheme. The Gram Panchayat at village level and Municipalities in urban areas are responsible for identifying persons eligible for the scheme.

Official information[1] indicates that in the year 2005-06, expenditure on Annapurna scheme in the country was about Rs. 1,394 lakhs and number of beneficiaries was 3,86,488. Further, Assam has 26,640 beneficiaries and the expenditure is about Rs. 204 lakhs. Bihar has more than five times the

1. *Source:* Annual Report, 2005-06, Ministry of Rural Development.

Table 8.4: Knowledge and Receipt of Annapurna Scheme (Percentages)

State	*Respondents Aware*			*Respondents receiving Annapurna*
	Elderly Women	*Care-givers*	*Stake-holders*	
Assam	24	27	93	2
Bihar	36	32	84	6
Chhattisgarh	12	15	90	2
Jharkhand	55	54	98	12
Madhya Pradesh	5	4	9	1
Orissa	37	34	94	6
Sikkim	46	32	84	5
Uttar Pradesh	22	31	84	2
Total	**29**	**29**	**79**	**4**

Table 8.4 shows that most of the stakeholders have heard of Annapurna scheme, except those hailing from Madhya Pradesh. Going back to Table 8.11, there is a certain lack of information on Annapurna Scheme in Madhya Pradesh. Similar is the awareness level of elderly women and their caregivers in the state about Annapurna scheme. Further, in Jharkhand maximum proportion of respondents in all the three categories — elderly women, their caregivers and stakeholders — have knowledge about Annapurna scheme.

Taken together, about 30 per cent of elderly women and similar proportion of their caregivers have knowledge about the Annapurna scheme. In the case of stakeholders, almost 80 per cent have information in this regard.

The Table 8.4 also provides the details of availing of Annapurna scheme by the elderly women. The highest proportion of elderly women availing Annapurna is from Jharkhand. This is corroborated by the findings that awareness regarding Annapurna is highest in Jharkhand and lowest in Madhya Pradesh. There is considerable difference in the proportion of elderly people knowing about the scheme and those availing it.

Not only is the reach of Annapurna scheme small, awareness is yet another factor to contend with. In the general opinion of the elderly women and the stakeholders, the quantity and the quality of the food grains distributed is below the level of satisfaction over which the attention of the policy makers needs to be focused.

Old Age Pension

As a part of economic security, social assistance is provided to the needy elderly. It is a centrally sponsored scheme by the name of National Old Age Pension Scheme where assistance of Rs. 200 per month is given to destitute elderly through the state concerned. Attached to the scheme are, however, a few eligibility conditions. These include domicile, sex-age proof and absence of close relatives. May it be noted that the proportion of the elderly persons receiving NOAP varies from state to state. Apparently, states like Haryana, Goa, Himachal Pradesh, Manipur, are somewhat liberal, in that a sizeable proportion of aged persons have the benefit of NOAP, others accord the scheme a rather low priority.

Table 8.5: State-wise number of beneficiaries covered under National Old Age Pension Scheme

State	*2000-2001*	*2005-06**
Assam	2,62,719	2,99,005
Bihar	5,09,938	4,82,212
Chhattisgarh	1,46,519	1,82,621
Jharkhand	1,75,437	41,511
Madhya Pradesh	4,29,490	6,83,680
Orissa	3,84,174	4,93,187
Sikkim	10,104	10,104
Uttar Pradesh	8,41,340	12,61,094
Total	**51,48,226**	**56,72,749**

Source: Handbook on Social Statistics, Ministry of Social Justice and Empowerment, 2004 and Ministry of Rural Development, Annual Report 2005-06.

Table 8.5 gives the details of number of beneficiaries under the National Old Age Pension (NOAP) Scheme for the years 2000-2001 and 2005-06. Uttar Pradesh has maximum number of beneficiaries, followed by Madhya Pradesh with almost a half of the number of beneficiaries than the former state. It may be noted that in Madhya Pradesh, NOAP is quite popular unlike Annapurna scheme. This may be attributed to better reach and coverage of NOAP that makes the complementary scheme — Annapurna — not very popular.

Apart from the National Old Age Pension Scheme, many states have their own OAP scheme. Data bring out that rate of old age pension in the states under study varies from Rupees 75 to Rupees 200 per month. Assam and Chhattisgarh have Rs. 75 as Old Age Pension, Sikkim and Bihar have Rs. 100, Uttar Pradesh has the rate of Rs. 100 and Orissa has the maximum of 200 rupees. State-wise variations are also observed in the number of beneficiaries availing OAP, while, Bihar has 301455 beneficiaries, Orissa has 675000. Also, except Uttar Pradesh, wherever, information could be gathered in all the states the proportion of female beneficiaries is higher than that of males beneficiaries.

Table 8.6: State-wise Old Age Pension Amount and Minimum Age

State	*Pension Amount (Rs/Month)*	*Minimum Age (Years)*
Assam	75	65 (male) and 60 (female)
Bihar	100	60
Chhattisgarh	75	65
Jharkhand	200	60
Madhya Pradesh	150	65 (male) & 60 (female)
Orissa	150	65
Sikkim	200	-
Uttar Pradesh	125	60

Source: Geriatric Care – A User, Friendly Document. NSID, Ministry of SJE, 2004.

Table 8.6 brings out the state-wise variations in age as criterion for providing old age pension. In Uttar Pradesh, Jharkhand and Bihar, it is in corroboration with National Policy on Older Persons to regard a person aged 60 years or more as elderly. In Madhya Pradesh and Assam, we observe some kind of gender sensitivity as age criterion is lowered to 60 years for females.

Table 8.7 brings out the awareness level and beneficiaries of the schemes among respondents in the three categories about Old Age Pension. It shows that most of the stakeholders know about the Old Age Pension scheme for them and elderly in Madhya Pradesh having highest awareness level. On the whole, most of the stakeholders are aware of the OAP scheme and more than 80 per cent of elderly women are also aware while only two-thirds of the caregivers have information about it.

Table 8.7: Knowledge about Old Age Pension Scheme (Percentages)

State	*Awareness Level*			*Respondents availing OAP*
	Elderly Women	*Care Givers*	*Stake-holders*	
Assam	88	86	97	27
Bihar	85	72	95	21
Chhattisgarh	64	39	99	22
Jharkhand	89	75	98	22
Madhya Pradesh	96	76	89	25
Orissa	80	56	99	30
Sikkim	87	53	96	31
Uttar Pradesh	68	70	92	10
Total	**82**	**66**	**95**	**23**

Table 8.7 shows that 23 per cent of respondents are availing Old Age Pension. Lowest proportion of respondents availing OAP is from Uttar Pradesh while highest is from Sikkim.

Orissa too has a high proportion of elderly women availing OAP.

At this juncture, the data gathered during FGDs with stakeholders may be drawn upon. Panchayat members in Betul, Madhya Pradesh, consider that Old Age Pension of Rs.150 a month is hardly sufficient for destitute elderly women to manage even two meals a day. Various government officials, NGO functionaries, panchayat leaders have maintained that the eligibility criterion of 'destitution' or no kith/kin to look after should be done away with. Many grown up children do not care for their elderly parents and state also does not intervene believing that the family would take care of the elderly. So, OAP should be given to all the elderly people irrespective of their family's condition.

During FGDs, with stakeholders it has come out that in Development Block Hiswa, Nawada, Bihar, no elderly person has ever being granted OAP since Independence. Much of this is attributed to the apathy of the PRIs and government officials.

Many elderly women, during FGDs, emphasised that though there are several government schemes but they are unable to avail them, because officials ask for bribe. They demanded that something should be done to curb corruption. During data collection, field researchers have also found that even doctors are asking for Rs.100 (bribe) to certify ages to destitute and poor elderly women, which is a requirement for applying for OAP or Annapurna.

Day Care Centres

Sometimes called hobby clubs, activity-centres, recreational centers, golden age centers, Day Care Centre (DCC) scheme was started in the late Eighties. With the financial assistance of Ministry of Social Justice and Empowerment, these centers are being run by voluntary agencies, in almost all the states.

In the study 98 per cent stakeholders denied the presence of day care centres for the elderly in their area. Only two per cent affirm existence of Day Care Centres. Especially in Assam, Bihar and Chhattisgarh, in the opinion of stakeholders, there are no Day Care Centres. Contrarily, the highest number and proportion of stakeholders confirm the presence of DCC in their areas. The number of DCCs, in all the study state, ranges from one to nine only. The stakeholders are further asked if there is no DCC in their area/district, have any NGOs tried setting up the same. Only 2.8 per cent affirmed that NGOs have tried so and only 1.9 per cent report that NGOs tried getting grants from Ministry of Social Justice and Empowerment for setting up DCC in their respective areas.

Data bring out that only one per cent elderly respondents have heard of Day Care Centres and slightly lower is the proportion of their caregivers (0.7 per cent) are knowing about this facility. Further data show that merely 0.4 per cent elderly know of someone availing the services of DCC. However, when asked if DCC is set up, would elderly respondents participate, 58 per cent respond in the affirmative.

Data analysis gives the impression that many people, including elderly are not aware of the Day Care Centres scheme. During FGDs too, stakeholders show a lack of awareness regarding DCC. Many stakeholders are willing to establish such facilities - chairperson of Rajput Gram Udhyog Samiti, a community based organisation in the Jhansi district of Uttar Pradesh, is among many NGO functionaries who intend to run a Day Care Centres in their area for elderly women. Regional variations have also surfaced during FGDs. In Cuttack, Orissa, elderly women are active participants in the three DCCs being run in the district while elderly women of Ganjam (Orissa) hardly know about their existence.

Old Age Homes

The Concept of old age homes is not very popular in the subcontinent. Much of it could be traced to the tradition that it is the responsibility of family to care for their elderly relatives. However, for many older persons who have nowhere to go and no one to support them, old age homes serve as a haven. While these homes do discharge an important function, there are also several limitations, which make them a poor substitute for family. Many studies have shown that institutionalisation has negative effect on the well-being of the elderly in India (Ramamurti and Jamuna, 1991; Chadha, 1995).

In the present study it is seen that awareness about the

existence and availability of Old Age Homes among elderly women is noticeably low (eight per cent). This kind of awareness is a shade better among caregivers and stakeholders (see table 8.8).

About 13 per cent stakeholders confirm the existence of old age homes in the district. In a few states like Assam and Bihar, none of the stakeholders report the existence of any old age home. In Madhya Pradesh and Chhattisgarh nearly a third of the stakeholders affirm the presence of such homes in their area.

Table 8.8 : State-wise distribution of Knowledge about Old Age Homes (Percentages)

State	*Respondents*	
	Elderly Women	*Care Givers*
Assam	6	13
Bihar	3	4
Chhattisgarh	4	8
Jharkhand	12	6
Madhya Pradesh	6	19
Orissa	4	5
Sikkim	9	15
Uttar Pradesh	16	11
Total	**8**	**10**

Data further show that only one per cent respondents know someone staying in an old age home. Only 0.7 per cent the elderly women (number 51) have tried admission in an old age home. When asked, if needed, would the respondents be willing to get admitted in a home, nearly a-third of elderly women have shown willingness (others are unwilling).

In Chhattisgarh and Madhya Pradesh old age home is less popular among elderly women and their caregivers. This is not shown in Bihar and Sikkim. Qualitative data collected through FGD show that many districts like Cuttack in Orissa have a good number of old age homes and others like

Kabirdham (in Chhattisgarh), Sonitpur (in Assam) have none. Further, NGO and government functionaries said that about 98 per cent of elderly women are not willing to get admitted into old age homes. However, there is a need for at least one Old Age Home in each district for poor and deserted elderly women.

One village Sarpanch in Cuttack, Orissa, reflects that there are a few old age homes but most people are not even aware of these. One teacher in, Goalpara, Assam, says, "Most of the people are not willing to send their parents to old age homes because it lowers their prestige and status."

Ministry of Social Justice and Empowerment Government of India, during 2004-05 has released an amount of Rs 15.68 Crores to 444 NGOs for running 338 Old Age Homes, 241 Day Care Centres, 45 Mobile Medicare Units and 2 non-institutional service centers which would benefit 55,550 older persons.

CIVIL SOCIETY INITIATIVES AND OTHER SPONSORED PROGRAMMES

Apart from the schemes mentioned above, Ministry of Social Justice and Empowerment, Government of India, funds two more programmes.

Integrated Programme for Older Persons: Under this scheme financial assistance up to 90 per cent of the project cost is provided to NGOs for establishing and maintaining old age homes, day care centres, mobile medicare units and other non-institutional services to older persons.

The scheme has been made flexible so as to meet the diverse needs of older persons including reinforcement and strengthening of the family-bonds, awareness generation on issues pertaining to older persons, popularisation of the concept of life-long preparation for old age, facilitating productive ageing, etc. The budget allocation during 2005-2006 was Rs. 19.80 crores and the revised expenditure was Rs. 14.00 crores. The budget allocation for the year 2006-07 has been kept at Rs. 28 crores.

Civil society organisations, particularly voluntary organisations have played a crucial role in implementing welfare and development programmes for disadvantaged sections of the society, including the elderly. Table 8.23 provides details of assistance given to voluntary organisations working for the welfare and well-being of the elderly. It brings out that financial outlay, revised expenditure and expenses are somewhat decreasing. Despite the fact that the numbers of elderly is increasing in the country, and majority of the elderly require assistance outside families, the trend of decreasing fund allocation and expenditure causes concern.

Scheme of Assistance to Panchayati Raj Institutions/ Voluntary Organisations/Self Help Groups for the Construction of old age homes/multi service centres for older persons.

This scheme provides for one time construction grant for old age homes/multi service centers. Registered societies, public trusts, Charitable Societies or registered Self-help Groups of Older Persons in addition to Panchayati Raj Institutions are eligible to get financial assistance under this scheme. Against the budget allocation during 2005-06 of Rs.67 lakhs, the expenditure was Rs. 47 lakhs. Here again a lot of flexibility has been given to these bodies of grass-roots governance and civil society organisations. Also, government is trying all the civil society organisations interested to work for the older persons to seek grant and implement need-based programmes, which are tailor-made to suit the local geographical and socio-cultural milieu.

Official figure says that in 1998-99, Rs.155 lakh were allocated for the scheme of assistance to PRI/VO/SHG and the like. Then, in the year 1999-2000, it was increased to nearly Rs.236 lakhs. However, in the year 2000-01, it was merely 72 lakhs, then subsequently, in the following year, it was increased to Rs. 113 lakhs. This trend is rather disheartening and signifies either lack of information to civil society organisations about the scheme or hurdles in getting the grant processed at various levels.

The data further show that in Bihar, Jharkhand, Madhya Pradesh and Sikkim, the scheme has never arrived in the states, while in Uttar Pradesh and Orissa, recently no civil society organisations are there to avail of the scheme.

Help Age India Initiatives

Along with the government, many civil society bodies have come up to work for the welfare and well-being of older persons the country-wide. Help Age-India stands out among them. Others are Age Care-India, Gerontological Association of India, Age-Well Foundation, Dignity Foundation and Society for Gerontological Research, to mention a few.

This apart, many schools, mostly independent, through their 'socially useful and productive work', and schools of social work, function to inculcate inter-generational cordial relationship through such programmes as celebrating Annual Day as Grandparents day, Adopt a Granny programmes and the like.

Help Age India was established in 1978 to work nation wide for the cause and care of the elderly people, with its head office in New Delhi. It has its regional centers in almost all the major cities of the country. It has also become a funding organisation along with implementing most programmes itself. Besides creating awareness among the people about the needs and problems of the elderly in the society, it also funds many day care centers, old age homes, geriatric wards, mobile care units, conducting cataract operations, income-generating programmes for elderly to describe some.

Besides, Help Age India is also providing technical expertise for age care projects. Since its inception, the organisation has sponsored more than 700 such projects with a total outlay of about Rs. 10 crores. 'Adopt a Granny' scheme intends to provide rehabilitation at the door-steps of elderly women. For raising funds, Help Age cards, sponsorship request letters, organising events, and making films are the main strategies. Research into gerontological concerns has also been the salient activity of Help Age India.

These are some of the prominent social security measures taken up by the government and civil society organisations. It is observed that some efforts have been made to implement the vision and objectives mentioned in the National Policy on Older Persons, 1999, that commits the nation to work for the care, security, participation, dignity and independence of our senior citizens but these measures are not enough for their upliftment. A systematic intervention is required to reduce risk factors of elderly women and to shield them from vulnerability.

9

Conclusion and Recommendations

For several pressing and pertinent reasons, gerontological issues have, in recent decades, started attracting the attention of policy-makers and programme-planners. As is well known, the proportion of the elderly in general population has increased and is increasing fast, mainly on account of improvement in nutrition and rapid strides in medical technology. This apart, cultural, economic and social structure has undergone radical changes. As a consequence, traditional support systems for the aged have become markedly less effective, necessitating alternatives and substitutive institutions.

Should we consider gerontological issues along with gender issues, the matter becomes more complex and serious. It goes without saying that, for several historical and cultural reasons, women have had social status less than equal to that man. Aggregate data are emphatic and recurrent that women lag behind men in matters of health, education, and participation in work and community affairs. It is thus hardly surprising that, in most developing societies; elderly women are dependent (on husband or son) and vulnerable (to exigencies and hazards).

In this connection, much thinking has taken place all around. In 1982, under the aegies of the United Nations, World Assembly on Ageing articulated and recommended the concept of 'active ageing'. In 1991, the UN set forth five principles for evolving policies and programmes for aged people. These included independence, participation, care, fulfilment and dignity. These principles have been further elaborated, in 2002, at the United Nations World Assembly on Ageing held at Madrid.

The demographic scene in India is also undergoing rapid and radical changes. Census data show a clear upswing in the population of the aged. In this, the population growth of elderly women (age 60 years and more) stands out, perhaps because of several physiological and constitutional reasons.

On the other hand, as argued earlier, they are face-to-face with a variety of exigencies or vulnerable situations. These may include mainly bio-psychological vulnerability, economic vulnerability and socio-cultural vulnerability.

In relation to aged people, existing scientific literature does shed light on ageing and the aged, nutrition and health, social milieu, and economic conditions. We also have some information on social security and social assistance programmes in India. However, few studies have addressed the issue of vulnerability among elderly people, in general, and among elderly women, in particular. The work in hand is an attempt to bridge this information-gap.

The present study aims to look into and analyse risks-factors underlying vulnerability among the elderly women. These include social and economic status of elderly women, their nutritional status, physical and mental health and access to medical care facilities, and social interactional patterns. It also focalises existing governmental and non-governmental programmes as also their access to elderly women, in order to curve and control vulnerable conditions. Subsequently, the work makes a few data-based recommendations, which when implemented in spirit and letter, are likely to substantially limit vulnerable conditions confronted by elderly women.

In this regard, attention has been paid to those states in the country, which have a high 'below poverty line' (BPL) population. Thus, eight states (BPL ranging from 31 to 47 per cent) have been selected for the study. Districts in these states have been grouped under north, south, east, west zones, and from each zone one district has been selected. In turn, from each selected district two blocks primarily rural in character, and two towns (urban areas) have been picked up. Key informants, that is, elderly women and their caregivers have been selected on the basis of information in 'voter lists'.

Apart from official information, a large body of primary data has been collected from elderly women, caregivers and stakeholders. This has been supplemented by focus group discussions (FGD). Thus, the database for the study comprises 15,170 interviews, 65 FGDs and 101 case studies. Interview data have been subjected to extensive computer analysis, and the rest to qualitative analysis. The findings of the study are as interesting as these are revealing.

Overview

At the outset, the background of elderly women may be brought under the focus, as it is likely to aid in the understanding their situation as also the risk factors that beset them. During the decade 1991-2001, the population of elderly women has increased by 47 per cent, as against 34 per cent that of elderly men. Feminization of ageing is apparent. At any rate, the population of the elderly in the study states is substantial and in conformity with the national trends. It ranges from 5.7 to 8.4 per cent of the general population. Similarly, in the districts it is between 5.5 and 9.4 per cent. Needless to add, it is increasing by the year.

While average age of the elderly women is 67 years, their husbands are older than them. In a way, the state of Sikkim has more of 'young' (60-64 Years) older persons, and Orissa has more of 'old old' (75 & above) persons. Perhaps nutrition of and health care in the mountainous states would do with some improvement.

Among the elderly women, 85 per cent are those who profess Hinduism. This apart, the states of Orissa, Chhattisgarh, and Madhya Pradesh have more of Hindus. On the other hand, Assam, Uttar Pradesh, and Bihar have a sizable proportion of Muslims. May it be noted that Madhya Pradesh has large segment of those belonging to Schedule Castes. Similarly, Sikkim and Chhattisgarh have a large number of elderly women who belong to various Schedules Tribes.

Marital status is a significant consideration, particularly for women. It is observed that two elderly women out of every five are married. The rest are mostly widows. Among other things, this is indicative of the practice of men marrying women younger to them in age. Also this underlines a condition conducive to vulnerability.

As would be expected, illiteracy is widespread among the elderly women. Between 79 and 93 per cent of them have never being to school. Sates of Bihar, Chhattisgarh, Madhya Pradesh, and Uttar Pradesh have the dubious distinction of having nearly all the elderly women who are illiterate. At any rate, illiteracy clearly adds to vulnerability.

As per study design, a third of the elderly women are from urban areas and the rest from rural areas. It therefore falls into a pattern that nearly 60 per cent of family groups are either joint families or extended families. The trend is further reinforced by the fact that elderly women are from relatively large households (average, over 5 members), and that quite a few of them have a large number of sons and daughters. In a way, living arrangements are satisfactory as more than 95 per cent of the elderly women are found to be living with their natural families. These factors are likely to have a linkage with the vulnerability among the elderly women.

In any consideration of risk factors, livelihood issues figure prominently. These have a bearing on need-gratification, as also on the sense of security of the elderly women. As would be anticipated, elderly women covered by the study are mostly housewives or non-workers. Their proportion ranges in the study states from 51 per cent to 71 per cent. It is therefore hardly surprising that aggregate National Sample Survey data show more than 70 per cent of women, both in rural and urban areas, are dependent upon others. Nonetheless, some of the elderly women in the study do manage to raise some income, under rupees six hundred a month, with wide variation. Their husbands, reportedly, do a shade better, that is, over Rs. 1300 a month on an average. Taken together, average family income works out to be about Rs. 2700, with wide variations. Income data hardly speak well of economic security for the elderly women under study.

Of course, there is a large segment of the elderly women who are pensioners. However, only 13 per cent of them are in this category. Mean pension amount is found to be Rs. 1,389 per month. Is it adequate?

The study reveals that one elderly woman out of every seven has an account either in commercial bank or in post-office. An equal proportion has sundry sources of income, including remittance from sons and daughters or other close relatives. Many of them also have immovable property, including the house they live in. Some of them have income-yielding assets. However, the situation remains hardly encouraging, when the ownership of immovable assets is assessed: Only one out of every six elderly women has property in her name. The situation unequivocally speaks of their economic vulnerability.

The study also examines the expenditure pattern in the family groups of the elderly women. About a fourth of the elderly women pay for their upkeep to the households. Nearly 57 per cent of them state that several expenses concerning them are held up for want of money. Quite a few of them state that they cannot incur expenses on clothing, medicine and *dan-dakshina* on their own. Further, more than a half of them feel that the family group pays for their expenses, but reluctantly or even unwillingly. These data-positions unmistakably converge on economic vulnerability of the elderly women. This trend draws further support from the position that a large number of elderly women are interested in taking up some income generating activities.

With regard to elderly people, nutrition and health make for important risk factors in vulnerability. Indeed, ageing bring in its wake irreversible physiological changes. Health vulnerability is, thus, inherent in the situation. Nevertheless, several nutrition and health factors could be controlled or regulated to minimise vulnerability. To illustrate, most elderly women, caregivers and stakeholders state that nutrition of the elderly women suffers for want of money. On the other hand, balanced diet does not have to be necessarily, expensive diet. So, is the matter with healthy habits. Only one elderly woman out of every seven reportedly goes for a morning walk. This needs to be seen with the fact that quite a few of them require help in such daily life activities, as bathing, walking, etc.

As would be expected, a large number of elderly women report physical impairments. Their vision has gone down, their hearing has become hard or their bone joints have become stiff. Further, quite a few elderly women have reportedly developed persistent medical complaints. Mental health complaints are equally frequent. Elderly women complain of depression, anxiety, tension, insomnia and the like. Taken together, health vulnerability conditions among the elderly women are manifest. How about risk reduction?

When attention is paid to health facilities, a disquieting picture emerges. Reportedly, government hospitals are available, on an average, at a distance of four kilometers. This average is even larger for private hospitals. Only one elderly woman out of every six reports of a medical camp organized in her neighbourhood during the preceding year. Few elderly women know of the existence or visit of a mobile health unit in their area. On the others hand, they do need medical attention. During the preceding year, a large number of the elderly women have been hospitalized for one reason or the other. In any case, only 38 per cent of the elderly women have a favourable opinion about dispensaries or hospitals they have been to, and the rest of them have indifferent or even unfavourable opinion. The most critical risk factor, however, is the fact that a fifth of elderly women are neglecting or postponing the treatment of a long-standing medical problem.

Invisible and unquantifiable, interpersonal relations are quintessential in a consideration of vulnerability among the aged. As pointed out earlier, social matrix has, in modern times, undergone radical changes. The situation calls for appropriate and effective adjustment or readjustment between the elderly and the family and the community, and for setting up of social services, both institutional and non-institutional on some scale. We, therefore, need to take a close look at interpersonal relations, with a view to identifying risk factors behind social vulnerability.

Participation in household activities has both substantive and symbolic values. However, elderly people seldom appreciate this simple fact. In the context of elderly women, household chores would include, kitchen work, washing and mending of clothes, minding of infants and toddlers, etc.

It is seen that more than a third of them do not participate in these and similar activities on their own. Similarly, three-fourths of them do not interact with their neighbours. This hardly speaks well of their adjustment in the family or community. As a result, this is bound to get reflected on their social vulnerability.

A pointed attention has been paid to the widows. It would be recalled that more than 60 per cent of the elderly women under study are in this category. As their social interactional pattern seems to undergo several changes after widowhood.

A significant proportion of elderly women respond in the affirmative: Regard and respect to them has gone down. Food, clothing, and medical care have got neglected, and their social visits to their neighborhood have become fewer. Furthermore, around a fifth of them after widowhood often face unwarranted shouting, pushing or beating. Needless to add, widowhood positively adds to social vulnerability.

This apart, social integration of elderly women presents a mixed picture. It is observed that sons and daughters are comparatively more deferential towards them than sons-in-laws and daughter-in-laws. A third or more of them are not consulted in familial decision-making, including in food preparation, rearing of grandchildren, assets transactions etc. More than a half of them do not have an exclusive room to themselves, and have to make do with shared accommodation or even with a verandah or barsati. Rude behavior by family members towards the elderly women is not unheard of. Many of them are ignored or neglected, subjected to abusive languages or denied food, medicine etc. A few of them also report to have been slapped, beaten or thrown, temporarily, out of the house.

Having outlined the risk factors impacting on economic, health and social vulnerability, an attempt has been made to evolve a holistic view. Towards this, Scalogram technique has been adopted to develop composite variables.

Assessment of Economic Vulnerability brings out that about a fourth of elderly women are highly vulnerable. It tends to increase with age. Perhaps with advancing age need-pattern changes and dependency increases.

It is observed that in rural areas, the likelihood of moderate and high economic vulnerability is more than in urban areas. This could be explained in terms of the availability of civic amenities and opportunity structures. Economic vulnerability has also been examined in terms of states under study. It is seen that Sikkim and Madhya Pradesh are relatively better off. In contrast, Bihar, Chhattisgarh and Uttar Pradesh have elderly women exposed to 'high' economic vulnerability, may be this has something to do with GDP and per capita income in these states.

In the context of ageing and aged, the concept of health vulnerability is of paramount importance. Paying attention to nutrition, sensory impairment, handling of activities of daily life, physical condition and mental health problems, a composite variable Health Vulnerability has been generated. It is found that about 27 per cent of the elderly women are face-to-face with high health vulnerability. It is hardly surprising that health vulnerability and age are correlated: With age it tends to go up. But what is surprising is that there are no notable differences in respect of elderly women in rural areas and their sisters in urban areas. Perhaps health or ill health among the aged goes beyond civic amenities or health infrastructure. This aside, an attempt has been made to rank states in terms of Health Vulnerability. It is found that Madhya Pradesh occupies the lowest rank and Assam the highest. Stated differently, the elderly women in Assam are exposed to larger health vulnerability than their sisters in other states.

Next, attempt has been made to assess social vulnerability. Towards this, family decision-making, participation in household activities, abuse of the elderly women, and researchers' observation have been utilized to develop a composite variable Social Vulnerability. It is observed that a third of the elderly women are exposed to medium social vulnerability and a fourth to high vulnerability. Also, in the present case, there is observed a strong linkage between social vulnerability and age. Apparently, the elderly becomes socially more vulnerable as they advance in age. The possibility is strong that they start getting bypassed or being taken for granted. It is further observed that the state of Sikkim and Assam are relatively 'better off'; whereas Uttar Pradesh and Bihar show up in the category of high Social Vulnerability.

In order to develop a holistic view, economic, health and social vulnerability have been indexed into a composite variable, namely, Overall Vulnerability. It is seen that about 20 per cent of the elderly women have moderate overall vulnerability and about 31 per cent high vulnerability. As would be expected, single elderly women, including widows, unmarried and divorced women, are more exposed to high overall vulnerability. Probably in critical situations and exigencies, they are to fend for themselves in the relative absence of safety nets. As observed earlier, Overall Vulnerability too tends to escalate with age. It is interesting and relevant to examine the extent of Overall Vulnerability in the states under study. While Sikkim, Jharkhand and Madhya Pradesh are found to have low Overall Vulnerability; Uttar Pradesh and Bihar are assessed to have high Overall Vulnerability.

It may be remarked that states like Bihar, Chhattisgarh, Uttar Pradesh and Assam call for a concerted attention of policy makers to develop strategic interventions for rapid socio-economic change which would, among other things, protect the elderly from vulnerability.

In controlling risk factors and in reducing vulnerability, social support structure plays an incomparable role. Given this, the present work pays a concerted attention to this. In this connection, the views of 'stakeholders' have also been brought in. Only one stakeholder out of every six has information that the local hospital(s) has a 'geriatric unit'. According to them, two-thirds of the elderly people access government hospitals when they fall ill. Perhaps treatment in government hospitals and dispensaries is less expensive. Besides, in many areas, particularly in rural areas, it may be only Primary Health Centres, which would be available by way of medical facilities. According to about three-fourths of the stakeholders, the upcoming generation, that is, young boys and girls, are less respectful and deferential towards the aged than what they used to be a few decades ago. So, might be about the case with the grown-up sons and daughters in the maintenance of their elderly people. In this regard, according to 95 per cent of the stakeholders, Section 125 of the Code of Criminal Procedure has been ineffective. Many of them are aware of violence against the elderly and their opinion is that it is increasing.

The study takes a critical look at the ongoing social support schemes. In concept, Annapurna scheme is quite attractive. Country has a huge food-reserve that needs replacement year after year. Under the scheme, indigent aged persons are provided food grains, instead of cash. Relating to the year 2005-06, official figures indicate that, in the eight study states, 5,618 quintals of food grain has been distributed among 56,184 beneficiaries. It follows that the awareness about the scheme is somewhat sizeable: Many elderly women and their caregivers and several stakeholders know of it. And 22 per cent of the elderly women are benefiting from this scheme. FGDs and researchers, impressions, however, throw up two limiting conditions: Many eligible elderly persons have not been able to get approval for the scheme in spite of their repeated efforts; and the quality of food grains distributed under the scheme leaves much to be desired.

As known, we have Old Age Pension Scheme as well as National Old Age Pension. The latter is a 'centrally-sponsored' scheme. In some states, the two schemes have been combined. Pertaining to the study states, official figures indicate that, during 2005-06, nearly 56 lakhs elderly persons were availing of Old Age Pension. Field data go to show that the awareness level about Old Age Pension is quite high. Most of the elderly women, caregivers and stakeholders know about it. Further, 10 to 31 per cent of the elderly women in the study states are benefiting from the scheme. Again, this scheme has two main limiting conditions: Criteria for the grant of Old Age Pension are quite stringent; and the amount under the old age pension, in many states, is grossly insufficient to keep body and soul together.

Ministry of Social Justice & Empowerment, Government of India, supports Day Care Centres (DCC) set up by non-governmental organizations. The number of DCCs is between

300 and 350, spread all over the country. The numerical insufficiency of the DCCs is obvious. It is, therefore, hardly surprising that very few elderly women, caregivers and stakeholders have heard of Day Care Centres. Nonetheless, more than a half of the women would be willing to participate, should a Day Care Centre be set up in their neighbourhood.

All said and done, there would be many elderly, who would require institutional care for reasons more than one. In the study states, there are functional 93 Old Age Homes. It is, therefore, surprising that only around a tenth of the elderly women and their caregivers know of Old Age Homes.

Similarly, only a third of the elderly women are interested in seeking admission to a Home and less than a fourth of the caregivers are willing to send their elderly to a Home. Among other things, the lack of interest in the institutions for the elderly is indicative of social ethos and family bonding.

While discussing support structure, a mention needs to be made of government assistance to NGOs providing institutional and non-institutional services to the elderly. Under the Tenth Five-Year Plan, an allocation of Rs. 19.8 crores has been made.

The foregoing brings out some of the initiatives evolved to tackle risk factors, and to make a dent into the problem of vulnerability of the elderly women. Apparently, some distance has been covered in this direction but much more remains to be covered.

Suggestions

Keeping in view the demographic, economic, social and health changes impacting on the ageing and the aged, a few recommendations could be put forth for the consideration of policy makers and programme planners.

Socio-cultural Initiatives

1. Following from a marked shift from agrarian society to industrial society, and from joint family to nuclear family system, implications for the lifestyle of the elderly are serious. This calls for the setting up of a chain of substitutive institutions, for providing care to the elderly at the neighbourhood or village level.

2. In view of the rapidly changing social scenario, elderly women as well as their family members should be given individual and group counseling for promoting proper and healthy adjustment at the family level.
3. In the study, many elderly women have reported that they are subjected to harsh treatment, even to abuse, by their grown-up children and their spouse. In this context, media campaigns should be developed and launched for spreading awareness of the provisions under Section 125 of Code of Criminal Procedure, Himachal Pradesh Maintenance of Parents Act, and Domestic Violence Act, 2005. These campaigns may also highlight judgments under these Acts pronounced by superior courts.
4. Government and private schools, as part of the co-curricular activity, Socially Useful and Productive Work, may take up the responsibility to inculcate values and respect for elderly persons - by organizing regular visits to Old Age Homes and Day Care Centres, and encouraging students to actively participate in 'Adopt a Granny' programme.
5. In order to inculcate sensitivity in the masses towards the elderly, Elders Day, Parents Day, Centurions Day and the like may be organised.

Economic Issues

6. A vast majority of elderly women in the study have been found to be non-workers and economically dependent. For this, feasible Income-generating schemes should be formulated for providing physically less demanding work for the self-employment of the elderly women, so as to reduce their economic dependence.

   Towaqrds this, in each district, an established and reputed NGO should be appointed to work as a Facilitator for elderly women. Main activities of the NGO may be as follows:

   - Conducting feasibility study for selecting Income Generating Activities (IGA).
   - Motivating elderly women to take-up income generating activities.

- Organizing training programmes for skill development.
- Assisting them in securing bank-loan, and in the marketing of goods and services produced by them.

Towards encouraging the participation of the elderly women in salaried work, suitable for their age and past experiences, the NGO may act as a bridge between the them and prospective employers.

It is proposed that the Ministry of Social Justice and Empowerment, or Ministry of Women and Child Development should extend necessary support to the NGOs.

7. The study brings out that quite a few elderly women have immovable assets in their name. In order to rectify this situation, policy level measures should be undertaken to encourage the husbands to have property in the name of their spouse, by giving them tax relief and various other benefits.

Nutrition and Health

8. At the policy level, ICDS programme may initiate a provision for providing adequate nutritious food to the elderly women belonging to the BPL families. This is likely to greatly help the elderly women to have proper and nutritious food on low cost within the existing infrastructure, particularly in rural and tribal areas.
9. Focussed IEC campaigns may be designed and implemented to educate elderly women on the quality and quantity of healthy diet, in order to develop among them a proper understanding of balanced diet.
10. By networking with CSOs and NGOs, elderly persons should be educated to undertake regular light exercises, to ward off routine impairments and ailments. Further, yoga and meditation may become a part of the daily routine in Day Care Centres and Old Age Homes.
11. With a view to spreading health awareness among the elderly women, simple and readable print material may be designed, produced and widely distributed. Similarly,

wherever feasible, *nukkad natak*, *qawali*, magic shows, puppet shows, etc. should be organized to promote healthy and happy living among the elderly.

12. Geriatric care should form a part of National Rural Health Mission and may cover preventive, curative and disease management of health care.
13. Geriatric care unit should be established in all Primary Health Centres, district hospitals, and Old Age Homes to provide specialized medical care to elderly women.
14. Keeping in view the population distribution, especially in tribal and hilly areas, mobile health units should be set up and made operational as these are likely to benefit elderly women most on account of their lifestyle.
15. Elderly women should be allowed facilities of comprehensive medical check up at PHCs, CHCs and district hospitals, which would be a preventive measure, as also a reassuring measure. A provision for budget allocation should be made in this regard by the Planning Commission.
16. A fifth of the elderly women in the study are found to be neglecting or postponing treatment of outstanding symptoms or diseases. A modality should be evolved; perhaps in conjunction of CSOs and health volunteers, to reach out, identify such cases, and refer these to a PHC, district or regional hospital.
17. At the policy level, the Ministry of Health & Family Welfare, Government of India, should initiate a scheme on health insurance with affordable premium for catering to the medical needs of the elderly.

Interpersonal Relations

18. Training on family counseling should be imparted to ANMs, ASHA and Aaganwadi Workers. In turn, they would educate the elderly as well as the family members to maintain harmonious relations (with the elderly) at the family level.

    Such counseling sessions may also encourage elderly women to participate in the household chores within their physical and mental prowess.

19. Among elderly women the proportion of the widows is large and is likely to grow larger. On the other hand, they often face untoward situation in the family group. Awareness campaign should be planned to curb early marriages and reducing the huge gap of age between the husband and the wife.
20. Welfare agencies as well as non-governmental organizations, concerned with elderly welfare and development, should be directed to upgrade the interaction between the elderly and their community through self-helps groups, periodical meets, etc.

Social Support

21. Both in rural and urban areas, violence and other crimes against the elderly are reported to be increasing. Existing legal provisions need to be strengthened and, above all, they need to be vigorously implemented by the police and other public authorities.
22. District Social Welfare Officer and District Information Officer should be directed to disseminate information on various ongoing schemes meant for the elderly. These may develop IEC material such as booklets, leaflets, hoardings, etc., in simple regional language and distribute the material, perhaps through panchayats and municipal corporations.
23. Annapurna scheme should be implemented a little more liberally and vigorously by spreading mass awareness and by simplifying procedures, so that a larger number of elderly persons, including elderly women, particularly those in rural and tribal areas, are able to benefit from them.
24. In view of the food grain surplus in the country and of the directions of the Supreme Court of India, liberalisation of the Annapurna scheme is highly in order. Off setting food grain wastage, it would benefit a large number of elderly persons, including elderly women.
25. The distribution of food grains under the Annapurana scheme should be made more regular, and the quality of grains should be improved.

Appendices

NATIONAL POLICY ON OLDER PERSONS

(Formulated by the Govt. of India, Social Justice and Empowerment Ministry and adopted by the Union Cabinet on 13th February 1999)

I THE BACKGROUND

DEMOGRAPHIC TRENDS

1. Demographic Ageing : A global phenomenon has hit Indian shores as well. People are living longer. Expectation of life at birth for males has shown a steady rise from 42 years in 1951 - 60 to 58 years in 1986-90, it is projected to be 67 years in 2011-16, an increase of about 9 years in a twenty five year period (1986-90) to 2011-16), in the case of females, the increase in expectation of life has been higher, about 11 years, during the same period, from 58 years in 1986-90 to 69 years in 2011-16, At age 60 too, the expectation of life shows a steady rise and is a little higher for women. In 1989-93 it was 15 years for males 16 years for females.
2. Increased life expectancy has contributed to an increase in the number of persons 60+. From only 12 million persons 60+ in India in 1901, the number crossed 24 million in 1951 and 57 million in 1991. Population projections for 1996-2016 made by the Technical group on population projections (1996) indicate that the 100 million mark is expected to be reached in 2013. Projections beyond 2016 made by the United Nations (1996) Revision), has indicated that India will have 198 million persons 60+ in 2020 and 326 million in 2050. The percentage of persons 60+ in the total population has

seen a steady rise from 5.1 per cent in 1901 to 6.8 per cent in 1991. It is expected to reach 8.9 per cent in 2016. Projections beyond 2016 made by United Nations (1996 Revision) has indicated that 2.1 per cent of the India Population will be 60+ by 2050.

3. Growth rate on a larger demographic base implies a much larger increase in numbers. The will be the case in the coming years. The decade 2001-11 is expected to witness an increase of 25 million persons 60+, which is equivalent to the total population of persons 60+ in 1961. The twenty five year period from 1991 to 2016 will witness an increase of 55.4 million persons 60+, which is nearly the same as the population of persons 60+ in 1991. In other words, in the twenty five year period starting from 1991, the population 60+ will nearly double itself.
4. Sixty three per cent of the old population in 1991 (36 million) is in the age group 60-69 years. Often referred to as young old or not so old, while 11 per cent (6 million) is in the age group 80 years and over i.e in the older old or very old category. In 2016, the percentage in those age groups will be almost the same, but the numbers are expected to be 69 million and 11 million respectively. In other words, close to six-tenths of the population 60-69 years can be expected to be in reasonably good physical and mental health, free of serious disability and capable of leading an active life. About one-third of the population 70-79 can also be expected to be fit for a reasonably active life. This is indicative of the huge reserve of human resource.
5. Men outnumber women in India even after age 60 (29 million males and 27 million females 60+ in 1991). This will continue to be the situation in 2016, when there will be an estimated 57 million males and 56 million females 60+.
6. Incidence of widowhood is much higher among females 60+ than among males of the same age group, because it is customary to get married to men older than them ny several years, also they do not remarry and live longer. There were in 1991, 14.8 million widowed females

60+ compared to 4.5 million widowed males. In other words, there were four times as many widow females as widowed males.

2. IMPLICATIONS

7. The demographic ageing of population has implications at the macro and also at household level. The sheer magnitude of numbers is indicative, both of the huge human reserve and also of the scale of endeavours necessary to provide social services and other benefits.
8. Demographic transition has been accompanied by changes in society and economy. These are of a positive nature in some areas and a cause of concern on others.
9. A growing number of persons 60+ in the coming decades will belong to the middle and upper income groups, be economically better of with some degree of financial security, have higher professional and educational qualifications, lead an active life in their 60s and even first half of 70s and have a positive frame of mind, looking for opportunities for a more active, creative and studying life.
10. Some areas of concern in the situation of older persons will also emerge, signs of which are already evident, resulting in pressures and fissures in living arrangements of older persons. It is true that family ties in India are very strong and an over whelming majority live with their sons or are suopported by them. Also, working examples find the presence of old persons, emotionally bonding and of great help in managing the household and caring for children. However, due to the operation of several factors, the position of a large number of older persons has become vulnerable due to which they cannot be taken for granted that their children will be able to look after them when they need care in old age, specially in view of the longer life span implying an extended period of dependency and higher costs to meet health and other needs.
11. Industrialization, urbanization, education and exposure to life style in developed countries bring in changes in

values and life styles. Much higher costs of bringing up and educating children and pressures for gratification of their desires affects transfer of shares of income for the care of parents. Due to shortage of space in dwellings in urban areas and high rents, migrants prefer to leave their parents in their native place. Changing roles and expectations of women, their concepts of privacy and space, desire not to be encumbered by caring responsibilities of old people for long periods, career ambitions, and employment outside the home implies considerably reduced time for care-giving. Also, adoption of small family norms by a growing number of families, daughters, too are fully occupied. Pursuing their educational career. The position of single persons, particularly females, is more vulnerable in old age as few persons are willing to take care for non-lineal relatives. So also is the situation of widows have no independent source or income, do not own assets and are totally dependent.

3. THE MANDATE

12. Well-being of older persons has been mandated in the Constitution of India. Article 41, Directive Principle of State Policy, has directed that the State shall, within the limits of its economic capacity and development, make effective provision for securities, the right to public assistance in case of old age. There are other provisions too, which direct the state to improve the quality of life of its citizens. Right to equality has been guaranteed by the Constitution as a Fundamental right. There provisions apply equally to older persons. Social security has been made the concurrent responsibility of the central and state Governments.

13. The last two decades have witnessed considerable discussions and debate on the impact of demographic transition and of changes in society and economy on the situation of older persons. The United Nations principle for Older persons adopted by the United Nations General Assembly in 1991, the Proclamations on Ageing and the Global targets as Ageing for the year 2001 adopted by

the General Assembly in 1992, and various other Resolutions adopted from time to time, are intended to encourage governments to design their policies and program in this regard.

14. There has for several years been a demand for a policy statement by the state towards its senior citizens so that they do not face an identity crisis and know where they stand in the overall national perspective. The need has been expressed at different forums where ageing issues has been deliberated. The statement, by indicating the principles underlying the policy, the directions, the needs that will be addressed and the relative roles of the government and non-government institutions, is expected to facilitate carving out of respective areas of operations, and action in the direction of a humane, age-integrated society.

II NATIONAL POLICY STATEMENT

15. The National policy, seeks to assure older persons that their concerns are national concerns and hey will not live unprotected, ignored or marginalized. The goal of the National Policy is the well - being of older persons. It aims to strengthen their legitimate place in society and help older persons to live their last phase of their life with purpose, dignity and peace.

16. The Policy visualizes that the state will extend support for financial security, healthcare, shelter, welfare and other needs of older persons, provide protection against abuse and exploitation, make available opportunities for the development of the potential and provide services so that they can improve the quality of their lives. The policy is based on some broad principles.

17. The Policy recognizes the need for affirmative action in favour of the elders. It has to be ensured that the rights of older persons are not violated and they get opportunities and equitable share in development program and administrative actions will reflect sensitivity towards older persons living in rural areas. Special attention will be necessary to older females so that they do not become

victims of triple neglect and discrimination on account of gender, widowhood and age.

18. The Policy views the life cycle as a continuous one of which past-60 phase of life is an integral part. It does not view age 60 as the cut off point for beginning a life of dependency. It considers 60+ as a phase when the individual should have the chances and opportunities to lead an active, creative, productive and satisfying life. An important thrust is, therefore, an active and productive involvement of older persons and not just their care.

19. The Policy values of an age-integrated society. It will endeavour to strengthen integration between generations, facilities two-way flows and interactions and strengthen the bonds between the young and the old. It believes in the development of social support system, informal as well as formal, so that the capacity of families to take care of older persons is strengthened and they can continue to live in their family.

20. The Policy recognizes that older persons too are a resource. They render useful service in the family and outside. They are not just consumers of goods and services, but also their producers. Opportunities and facilities need to be provided so that they can continue to contribute more effectively to the family, community and the society.

21. The policy firmly believes in the empowerment of older persons so that they can acquire better control over their lives and participate in decision-making on matters which affect them as well as the other issues as equal partners in the development process. The decision-making process will seek to involve them to a much larger extent, specially since they constitute 12 per cent of the electorate, a proportion which will rise in the coming years.

22. The Policy recognizes that larger budgetary allocations from the state will be needed and the rural and urban poor will be given special attention. However, it is neither

feasible nor desirable for the state alone to attain the objectives of the National Policy. Individuals, families, communities and institutions of civil society have to join hands as partners.

23. The Policy emphasizes the need for expansion of social and community services for older persons, particularly women, and enhance their accessibility and use by removing sociocultural, economic and physical barriers and making the services client-oriented and user-friendly. Special efforts will be made to ensure that the rural areas, where more than three-fourths of the older population lives, are adequately covered.

III PRINCIPAL AREAS OF INTERVENTION AND ACTION STRATEGIES

4. FINANCIAL SECURITY

24. A great anxiety in old age relates to financial insecurity. When the issue seen in the context of the fact that one-third of the population (1993-94) is below the poverty line and about one-third above it but belong to the lower income group, the financial situation of two-thirds of the population 60+ can be said to be fragile. Some level of income security in old age is goal which will be given very high priority. Policy instruments to cover different income segments will be developed.

25. For elderly persons below the poverty line, old age pensions provide some succor. Coverage under the old age pensions scheme for poor persons will be significantly expanded from the January, 1997 level of 2.76 million with the ultimate objective of covering all older persons below the poverty line. Simultaneously it will be necessary to prevent delays and check abuses in the matter of seletion and disbursement. Rate of monthly pension will need to be revised at intervals so that inflation does not deflate its real purchasing power. Simultaneously, the public distribution system will reach out to cover all persons 60+living below the poverty line.

26. Employees of government and quasi-government bodies and industrial workers desire better returns from

accumulations in provident funds, through prudent and safe investment of funds. Issues involved will be given consideration. It will be ensured that settlement of pensions, provident fund, gratuity and other retirement benefits is made promptly and superannuated persons are not put to hardship due to administrative lapses. Accountability for delays will be fixed. Redressal mechanisms for superannuated persons will be ensure prompt fair and humane treatment. Widows will be given special consideration in the matter of settlement of benefits accruing to them on demise of husband.

27. Pension is a much sought after income security. The base of pension coverage needs to be considerably expanded, it would be necessary to facilitate the establishment of pension scheme both in the private and in the public sector for self-employed and salaried persons in non-government employment with provision for employees also to contribute

28. Taxation polices will reflect sensitivity to financial problems of older persons, which accelerate due to very high costs of medical and nursing care, transportation and support services needed at home. Organization of Senior Citizens have been demanding a much higher standard deduction for then and standard deduction for them and a standard annual rebate for medical expenses treatment, whether domiciliary or hospital-based in cases where superannuated persons do not get medical coverage from their erstwhile employers. There are also demands, that some tax relief must be given to son of daughter when old parents co-reside and also allow some tax rebate of medical expenses. These and other proposal of tax relief will be considered.

29. Long term savings instruments will be promoted to reach both rural and urban areas. It will be necessary for the contributors to feel assured that the payments at the end of the stipulated period are attractive enough to take care of the likely erosion in purchasing power due to erosion. Earners will be motivated to save in their active working years for financial in old age.

30. Pre-retirement counseling programs will be promoted and assisted.

31. Employment in income-generating activities after superannuation should be the choice of the individual organizations which provide career guidance training and orientation and support services will be assisted. Programs of non-governmental organizations for generating income of old persons will be encouraged. Age-related discrimination in the matter of entitlement to credit marketing and other facilities will be removed. Structural adjustment policies may affect the older workers in some sectors more adversely. Specially those on household or small scale industry. Measures will be taken to protect their interests.

32. The right of parent without any means to be supported by their children having sufficient means has been recognized in Section 125 of the Criminal Procedure Code. The Hindu Adoption and Maintenance Act, 1956 too secures this right to parents. To simplify the procedure provide speedy relief, lay down the machinery for processing cases and define the rights and circumstances in a comprehensive manner, the Himachal Pradesh Maintenaces of Parents and Dependent bill, 1996. The Government of Maharashtra has prepared a Bill on similar lines. Other States will be encouraged to pass similar legislation so that old parents unable to maintain themselves do not face abandonment and acute neglect.

5. HEALTHCARE AND NUTRITION

33. With advancing age, old persons have to cope with health and associated problems some of which may be chronic, of a multiple nature, requires constant attention and carry the risk of disability and consequent loss of autonomy. Some health problems, specially when accompanied by impaired functional capacity require long term management of illness at home and of nursing care.

34. Health care needs of older persons will be given high priority. The goal should be affordable health services,

very heavily subsidized for the poor and graded system of user charges for others. It will be necessary to have a judicious mix of public health services, health insurance, health services provided by not-for profit organizations, including trusts and charities and private medical care. While the first of these will require greater State participation, the second category will need to be promoted by the state, the third category given some assistance, concessions and relief and the fourth encouraged, preferably by an association of providers of private care.

35. Primary health care system will be the basic structure of public healthcare. It will be basic structure of public healthcare. It will be strengthened and oriented to be able to meet the health care needs of older persons as well public health services, preventive, curative, restorative and rehabilitative, will be considerably expanded and strengthened and geriatric care facilities provided at secondary and tertiary levels. This will imply much larger public outlays, proper distribution of services in rural and urban areas and much better health administration and delivery systems.

36. The development of health insurance will be given high priority to cater to the needs of different income segments of the population and have provided for varying contributions and benefits. Package catering for the lower-income groups will be entitled to state subsidy. Various reliefs and concessions will be given to health insurance to enlarge the base of coverage and make them affordable.

37. Trusts, charitable societies and voluntary agencies will be promoted, encouraged and assisted by way of grants, tax relief and land at subsidized rates to provide free beds, medicine and treatment to the very poor elder citizens and reasonable user charges for the rest of the population.

38. Private medical care has expanded in recent years, offering the latest medical treatment facilities to those who can afford it. Where land and other facilities are

provided at less than market rates, bodies representing private hospitals and nursing homes will be requested to direct their members to offer a discount to older persons. Private general practitioners will be extended opportunities for orientation in geriatric care.

39. Public hospitals will be directed to ensure that elderly patients are not subjected to long waits and visits to different counters for medical tests and treatment. They will endeavour to provide separate counters and convenient timings on specified days. Geriatric wards will be set up.

40. Medical and paramedical personnel in primary secondary and tertiary health care facilities will be given training and orientation in health care of the elderly. Facilities for specialization in geriatrics medicine will be provided in the medical colleges. Training in nursing care will include geriatric care. Problems of accessibility and sue of health services by the elderly arise due to distance and absence of escort and transportation. Difficulties in reaching a public health mobile health services, special cases and ambulance services by charitable institutions and not for profit health care organizations. Hospitals will be encouraged to have a separate Welfare Fund, which will receive donations and grants for providing free treatment and medicines to poor elderly patients.

41. For the old who are chronically ill and are deprived of family support, hospitals supported or assisted by the state public charity and voluntary organizations will be necessary. These are also needed to cater to cases of abandonment to public hospitals.

42. Assistance will be given to geriatric care societies for the production and distribution of instruction material on self care by older persons. Preparation and distribution of easy-to-follow guidance material on health and nursing care of older persons for the use of the family care givers will also be supported.

43. Older persons and their families will be given access to educational material on nutritional needs in old age.

Information will be available on the foods to avoid and the right foods to eat. Diet receips suiting tastes of different regions and which are nutritious tasty, fit into the dietary pattern of the family and the community, are affordable and can be prepared from locally available vegetables, cereals and fruits will be disseminated.

44. The concept of healthy ageing will be promoted. It is necessary to educate older persons and their families that diseases are not a corollary of advancing age, nor is a particular chronological age the starting point for decline in health status. On the contrary, preventive health care and early diagnosis can keep a person in reasonable good health and prevent disability.

45. Health education programmes will be strengthened by making use of mass media and other communication channels, which reach out to different segments of the population. The capacity to cope with illness and manage lomiciliary care will be strengthened. Programs will also be developed targeting the younger and middle age groups to inform them how life styles during early years affect health status in late years. Messages on how to stay healthy for the entire life span will be given. The importance of balanced food diets, physical exercise, regular habits, reduction of stress, regular medical check up, allocation of time for leisure and recreation and pursuit of hobbies will be conveyed. Programs on Yoga, Meditation and methods of relaxation will be developed and transmitted through different channels of communication to reach diverse audiences.

46. Mental health services will be expanded and strengthened. Families will be provided counselling facilities and information on the care of treatment of older persons having mental health problems.

47. Non-governmental organizations will be encouraged and assisted through grants, training and orientation of their personnel and various concessions and relief to provide ambulatory services, day-care and health care to complement the efforts of the state.

48. Shelter is a basic human need. The stock of housing for different income segments will be increased. Housing schemes for urban and rural lower income segments will earmark 10 per cent of the houses, house-sites for allotment to older persons. This will include Indira Awas Yojana and other schemes of the Government. Earning persons will be motivated to invest in their housing in their earning days so that they have no problems of shelter when they grow old. This will require speedy urban land development for housing, time-bound provision of civic services and communication links, availability of loans at reasonable rates, easy repayment installments, time bound construction schedule and tax reliefs. Development of housing has to be a joint endeavour of public and private sectors and require participation of housing development boards, civic authorities, housing finance institutions and private developers and builders. Older persons will be given easy access to loans for purchase of housing and for major repairs, with easy repayment schedules.

49. Layouts of housing colonies will have to respond to the life styles of the elderly. It will have to be ensured that there are no physical barriers to mobility and accessibility to shopping complexes, community centres, parks and other service is safe and easy. A multipurpose centre for older persons is a necessity for special interaction and to meet other needs. It will therefore be necessary to earmark sites for such centres in all housing colonies. Segregation of older persons in housing colonies has to be avoided, as it prevents interaction with the rest of the community. Three or four storeyed houses without lifts are unfriendly to older persons, tend to isolate them, restrain their movement outside the home, and are a serious barrier to access to services. Preferences will be given to older persons in the allotment of flats on the ground floor.

50. Group housing of older persons, comprising of flatlets with common service facilities for meals, laundry, common room and rest room will be encouraged. Those

would have easy access to community services, media care parks, recreation and cultural centres.

51. Education, training and orientation of town planners, architects, and housing administrators will include modules on needs of older persons for safe and comfortable living.

52. Older Persons and their families will be provided of accidents and on measures which enhance safety, taking cognisance of reduced physical capacity and infirmities.

53. Noise and other forms of pollution affect children, the sick and older persons more adversely. Norms will be laid down and strictly enforced.

54. Civic authorities and bodies providing public utilities will be required to give top priority to attending to complaints of older persons. Payment of civic dues will be facilitated. Older persons will be given special consideration in promptly dealing with maters relating to transfer of property, mutation, property tax and other matters, harassment and abuses in such cases will be checked.

6. EDUCATION

55. Education, training and information needs of older persons will be met. These have received virtually no attention in the past. Information and educational material specially relevant to the lives of older people will be developed and widely disseminated using mass media and non-formal communication channels.

56. Discrimination, if any against older persons for availing opportunities for education, training and orientation will be removed. Continuing education programs will be encouraged and supported. These would cover a wide spectrum ranging from career development to recreation use of leisure and imparting skills in community work and welfare activities. Assistance of open universities will be sought to develop packages using distance education learning techniques. Access of older persons to libraries of universities, research institutions and cultural centres will be facilitated.

57. Educational curriculum at all stages of formal education as also non-formal education will incorporate material to strengthen inter- generational bonds and mutually supporting relationships. Interactions with educational institutions will be facilitated, whereby older persons with professional, qualifications and knowledge in science, arts, environment, socio - cultural heritage, sports and other areas could interact with children and young persons. Schools will encouraged and assisted to develop out-reach programs for interacting with older persons on a regular basis, participate in the running of senior citizens centres and develop activities in them.

58. Individuals of all ages, families and communities will be provided with information about the ageing process and the changing roles, responsibilities and relationships at different stages of the life cycle. The contributions of older persons inside the household and outside will be highlighted through the media and other forum and negative images, myths and stereotypes dispelled.

7. WELFARE

59. The main thrust of welfare will be to identify the more vulnerable among older persons such as the poor, the disabled, the infirm, the chronically sick and those without family support and provide welfare services to them on a priority basis. The policy will be to consider institutional care as the last resort when personal circumstances are such that their stay in old age homes becomes absolutely necessary.

60. Non-institutional services by voluntary organisations will be promoted and assisted to strengthen the coping capacity of the older persons and their families. This has become necessary, since families become smaller and women work outside the home, have to cope with scarcity of full-time care givers. Support services will provide some relief through sharing of the family's caring responsibilities.

61. Assistance will be provided to voluntary organisations by way of grants-in-aid for homes. Those for the poor will

be heavily subsided. It is important that such institutions become lively places of stay and provide opportunities to residents to interact with the outside world. Non-governmental organisations will be encouraged to seek professional expertise in the designing of old age homes, keeping in view needs of group living at this stage of the life cycle and the class of clients they serve. Minimum standards of services in such homes will be developed and facilities provided for training and orientation of persons employed in those homes.

62. Voluntary organisations will be encouraged and assisted to organise services such as daycare, multi-service citizen's centres, reach-out services, supply of disability related aids and appliances, assistance to old persons to learn to use them, short term stay services and friendly home visits by social workers. For old couples or persons living in their own, helpline, telephone assurance services, help in maintaining contacts with friends, relatives and neighbours and escorting older persons to hospitals, shopping complexes and other places will be promoted for which assistance will be given to voluntary organisations. Older persons will be encouraged to form informal groups of their own in the neighbourhood which satisfy the needs for social interaction, recreation and other activities. For a group of neighbourhood villages, the formation of senior citizen's forum will be encouraged.

63. A welfare fund for older persons will be set up. It will obtain funding support from government, corporate sector, trusts, charities, individual donors and others contributions to the fund will be given tax relief. States will be expected to establish similar funds.

64. The need for popularity of arrangements for welfare services in recognised government, voluntary organisations and private sector agencies, all have a place, the latter catering to those who have the means and desire better standards of care.

8. PROTECTION OF LIFE AND PROPERTY

65. Old persons become soft targets for criminal elements.

They also become victims of fraudulent dealings and of physical and emotional abuse within the household by family members to force them to part with their ownership rights. Widow's right of inheritance, occupancy and disposal at times, violated by their own children and relatives. It is important that protection is available to older persons. The introduction of special provisions in IPC to protect older persons from domestic violence will be considered and machinery provided to attend all such cases promptly. Tenancy legalisation will be reviewed so that the rights of occupancy of older persons are restored steadily.

66. Voluntary organisations and associations of older persons will be assisted to provide protective services and help to senior citizens through helping services, legal and other measures.

67. Police will be directed to keep a friendly vigil on older couples or old single persons living alone and promote mechanisms of interaction with neighbourhood associations. Information and advice will be made available to older persons on the importance of keeping contacts on phone with relatives, friends and neighbours and on precaution to be taken on matters such as prevention of un-authorised entry, hiring of domestic help, visits of repair and maintenance persons, vendors and others and the handling of cash and valuables.

9. OTHER AREAS OF ACTION

68. There are various other areas which would need affirmative action of the state to ensure that cards by the administration, fare concessions in all modes travel, preference in reservation of seats in local public transport, modification in the design of public transport vehicles for entry and exit, strict enforcement of traffic discipline at zebra crossings to facilitate older persons to cross streets, priority in gas and telephone connections and in fault repairs, removal of physical barriers to facilitate easy movement, concessions in entrance fee in leisure and entertainment facilities, art and cultural centres and places of tourist interest.

69. Speedy disposal of complaints of older persons relating to fraudulent dealings, cheating and other matters will go a long way in providing relief to them. Machinery for achieving this objective will be put in place.

70. Issues pertaining to older persons will be highlighted every year on the National Older Persons Day. The year 2000 will be declared as the National Year of Older Persons. Activities during the year will be planned and executed with the participation for different organisations.

71. Facilities, concessions and reliefs given to older persons by the central and state governments and other agencies will be compiled, updated at regular intervals and made available to associations of older persons for wide dissemination.

10. NON-GOVERNMENTAL ORGANISATIONS

72. The state alone cannot provide all the services needed by the older persons. Private sector agencies cater to a rather small segment of the population. The National Policy recognised the NGO sector as a very important institutional mechanism to provide user-friendly affordable services to complement the endeavours of the state in this direction.

73. Voluntary effort will be promoted and supported in a big way and efforts made to remedy the current uneven spread, both within a state and between states. There will be continuous dialogue and communication with NGO's on ageing issues and on services to be provided. Networking exchange of information and interaction among the NGOs will be facilitated. Opportunities will be provided for orientation and training of manpower. Transparency, accountability, simplification of procedures and timely release of grants to voluntary organisations will ensure better services. The grant-in-aid policy will provide incentives to encourage organisations to raise their own resources and not become dependent only on government funding and providing services on a sustainable basis.

74. Trusts, charities, religious and other endowments will be encouraged to extend their areas of concern to provide services to the elderly by involving them on ageing issues.

75. Older persons will be encouraged to recognise themselves to provide services to fellow senior citizens thereby making us of their professional knowledge, expertise and contacts. Initiative taken by them in advocacy, mobilisation of public opinion, raising of resources and community work will be supported.

76. Support will be provided for setting up volunteer programmes which will mobilise the participation of older persons and other in community affairs to interact with elders and help them with their problems. Volunteers will be provided opportunities for training and orientation on handling problems of the elderly and kept abreast of development in the field to promote active ageing. Volunteers will be encouraged to assist the home bound elderly, particularly frail and elderly women and help them to overcome loneliness.

77. Trade unions, employers' organisations and professional bodies will be approached to organise sensitivity programmes for their members on ageing issues and promote and organise services for superannuated workers.

11. REALISING THE POTENTIAL

78. The national policy recognises that 60+ phase of life is a huge untapped resource. Facilities will be made available so that the potential is realised and individuals are enabled to make the appropriate choices.

79. Older Persons, particularly women, perform useful but unsung roles in the household. Efforts will be made to make family members appreciate and respect the contribution of older persons in the running of the household specially when women too are working outside the home. Special programmes will be designed and disseminated through the media targeted at older persons so that they can enrich and update their knowledge, integrate tradition with contemporary needs and trasmit

more effectively socio cultural heritage to the grand children.

12. FAMILY

80. Family is the most-cherished institution in india and the most vital non-formal social security for the old. Most older persons stay with one or more of their children, particularly when independent living is no longer feasible. It is for them the most-preferred living arrangement and also the most emotionally satisfying. It is important that the family support system continues to be functional and the ability of the family to discharge its caring responsibilities is strengthened through support services.

81. Programmes will be developed to promote family-values, sensitise the young on the necessity and desirability of intergenerational bonding and continuity and the desirability of meeting filial obligations.Values of sharing and caring need to be reinforced. Society will need to be sensitised to accept the role of married daughters in sharing in the light of the changing context where parents have only one or two children in some situations only daughter. This would require some adjustment and changes in perception of in-laws in regard to sharing of caring responsibilities by some and daughters as a rollary to equal rights to inheritance and the greater emotional attachment the daughters have with their parents.

82. State policies will encourage children to co-reside with their parents by providing tax relief, allowing rebates for medical expenses and giving preferences in the allotment of houses. Parents will be encouraged to go in for long-term savings instrument and health insurance during their earning days so that financial load on families can be eased. NGOs will be encouraged and assisted to provide services which reach out to older persons in the home or in the community short term stay in facilities for older people will be supported so that families can get some relief when they go out. Counselling services will be strengthened to relieve intra-familial stresses.

13. SEARCH

83. The importance of a good data base on ageing will require to be strengthened. Univedrsities, Medical colleges and research institutions will be assisted to set up centres of gerontology studies and geriatrics. Corporate bodies, Banks, Trusts and endowments will be requested to institute chairs in universities and medical colleges in gerontological and geriatrics. Funding support will be provided to academic bodies for research projects on ageing. Superannuated scientists will be assisted so that their professional knowledge can be utilised.

84. An interdisciplinary co - ordinating body on research will be set up. Data collecting agencies will be requested to have a separate age category 60+ years and above. Professional association of gerontologists will be assisted to strengthen research activity, disseminate research findings and provide a platform for dialogue debate and exchange of information.

85. The necessity of a national institute of research, training and documentation is recognised. Assistance will be given for setting up research centres in different parts of the country.

14. TRAINING OF MANPOWER

86. The policy recognises the importance if trained manpower. Medical colleges will be assisted to offer specialities in geriatrics training institute for nurses and for the paramedical personnel need to introduce specific courses of geriatrics in their educational and training curriculum. In-service training centres will be strengthened to take up orientation courses on geriatric care. Assistance will be provided for development of curriculum and course material. Schools of social work and university departments need to give more attention to their curriculum to issues relating to older persons intervention strategies and organisations of services for them. Facilities will be provided and assistance given for training and orientation of personal non-governmental organisations providing service to older persons. Exchange of training personnel will be facilitated.

87. Assistance will be given for development and organisation of sensitation programmes on ageing for legislative, judicial and executive wings at different levels.

15. MEDIA

88. The National Policy recognises that media have a very important role to play in highlighting the changing situations of older persons and in identifying emerging issues and areas of action. Creative use of media can promote the concept of active ageing and help dispel stereo types and negative images about this stage of the life cycle. Media can also help to strengthen inter-generation bonds and provide individuals, families and groups with information and educational material which will give better understanding of the ageing process and of ways to handle problems as they arise.

89. The policy aims to involve media as well as informal and traditional communication channels on ageing issues. It will be necessary to provide opportunities to media personnel to have access to information apart from their aim independent sources of information and reporting of field situations. Their participation in orientation programmes on ageing will be facilitated. Opportunities will be extended for greater interaction between media personnel and persons active in the field of ageing.

IV. IMPLEMENTATION

90. The National policy on older persons will be very widely disseminated for which an action plan will be prepared so that its features remain inconstant public focus.

91. The policy will make a change in the lives of the senior citizens only if it is implemented. While the government and the principal organs have some basic responsibilities in the matter, other institutions as well as individuals will need to consider how they can play their respective roles for the well-being of older persons. Collaborative action will go a long way in achieving a more human society, which gives older persons their legitimate place. Apex level organisations of older persons have special responsibilities in this regard so that they can function

as a watchdog, energise continuing action, mobilise public opinion and generate pressure for implementaiton of the policy.

92. The ministry of social justice and empowerment will be the nodal ministry to coordinate all matters relating to the implementation of the policy. As separate bureau of older persons will be set up. An Inter-ministerial committee will coordinate matters relating to implementation of the national policy and monitor its progress. States will be encouraged to set up separate directorate of older persons and set up machinery for coordination and monitoring.

93. Five year and annual action plans will be prepared by each ministry top implement aspects which concern them. These will indicate steps to be taken to ensure flow of benefits to older persons from general programmes and from schemes specifically formulated for their wellbeing. Targets will be set within the framework of a time schedule. Responsibility for implementation of action points will be specified. The planning commission and the finance ministry will facilitate budgetary provisions required for implementation. The Annual report of each ministry will indicate progress achieved during the year.

94. Every three years the nodal ministry and orientation of personal non will prepare a detailed review - governmental organisations providing service to older persons. Exchange of training personnel will be facilitated.

95. Assistance will be given for development and organisation of sensitation programmes on ageing for legislative, judicial and executive wings at different levels.

15. MEDIA

96. The National policy recognises that media have a very important role to play in highlighting the changing situations of older persons and in identifying emerging issues and areas of action. Creative use of media can promote the concept of active ageing and help dispel stereotypes and nagative images about this stage of the life cycle. Media can also help to strengthen inter-

generation bonds and provide individuals, families and groups with information and educational material which will give better understanding of the ageing process and of ways to handle problems as they arise.

97. The Policy aims to involve media as well as informal and traditional communication channels on ageing issues. It will be necessary to provide opportunities to media personnel to have access to information apart from their aim independent sources of information and reporting of field situations. Their participation in orientation programmes in ageing will be facilitated. Opportunities will be extended for greater interaction between media personnel and persons active in the field of ageing.

V. IMPLEMENTATION

98. The National Policy on older persons will be very widely disseminated for which an action plan will be prepared so that its features remain inconstant public focus.

99. The policy will make a change in the lives of the senior citizens only if it is implemented. While the government and the principal organs have some basic responsibilities in the matter, other institutions as well as individuals will need to consider how they can play their respective roles for the well being of older persons. Collaborative action will go a long way in achieving a more human society, which gives older persons their legitimate place. Apex level organisations of older persons have special responsibilities in this regard so that they can function as a watchdog, energize continuing action, mobilize public opinion and generate pressure for implementation of the policy.

100. The ministry of social justice and empowerment will be the nodal ministry to co-ordinate all matters relating to the implementation of the policy. As separate bureau of older persons will be setup. An inter-ministerial committee will coordinate matters relating to implementation of the national policy and monitor its progress states will be encouraged to setup separate directorate of older

persons and set up machinery for coordination and monitoring.

101. Five year and Annual action plans will be prepared by each ministry to implement aspects which concern them. These will indicate steps to be taken to ensure flow of benefits to older persons from general programmes and from schemes specifically formulated for their wellbeing. Targets will be set within the framework of a time schedule. Responsibility for implementation of action points will be specified. The planning commission and the finance ministry will facilitate budgetary provisions required for implementation. The Annual report of each ministry will indicate progress achieved during the year.

102. Every three years a detailed review will be prepared by the nodal ministry on the implementation of the National policy. There will be non-official participation in the preparation of the document. The review will be a public document. It will be discussed in a National convention state government and union territories will be urged to take similar action.

103. An autonomous national council for older persons, headed by the minister for social justice and empowerment will be set up to persons. The council will include representatives of relevant central ministries and the planning commission. Five states will be represented on the council by rotation. Adequate representation will be given to non-official members representing non-government organizations, academic bodies, Media and experts on ageing issues from different fields.

104. An autonomous registered national association of older persons (NAOPs) will be established to mobilize senior citizens, particulate their interests, promote and undertake programs and activities for their wellbeing and to advise the government on all matters relation to older persons. The association will have national, state and district level officers and will choose its own office-bearers. The government will provide financial support to establish the national and state level offices while the district level offices will be established by the association

from its own resources, which may be raised through membership subscriptions, donations and other admissible means. The government will be able to provide financial assistance to the national and state level offices to cover both recurring as well as non-recurring administrative costs for a period of 15 years and thereafter the association is to be expected to be financially self-sufficient.

105. Panchayat Raj institutions will be encouraged to participate in the implementation of the national policy, address local levels issues and needs of the ageing and implement programs for them. They will provide forums for discussing concerns of older persons and activities that need to be taken. Such forums will be encouraged at Panchayat, block and district level. They will have adequate representation of older women. Panchayat will mobilize the talents and skills of older persons and draw up plans for utilizing these at the local level. Amongst others, the help of the social justice committees of the village panchayats will be taken to advocate different measures for giving effect to the policy.

106. In order to ensure effective implementation of the policy at different levels, from time to time the help of experts of public administration shall be taken to prepare the details of the organizational setup for the implementation, coordination and monitoring of the policy.

Bibliography

Adelmann, Pamela K. (1994): Multiple Roles and Physical Health among Older Adults: Gender and Ethnic Comparisons, *Research on Aging*, Vol. 16 (2), pp. 142-166.

Aiken, L.R. (1989): *Later life,* Hillsdale. New Jersey: Lawrence Erbium Associates.

Alam, Rafique and Husain, M.G. (1997): Psycho-Social Problems of Ageing: Indian Perspective in M G Husain (ed.); *Changing Indian Society and Status of Aged.* New Delhi; Manak Publication.

Anantharaman, R.N. (1990): Certain Associates of Physical Health in Old Age. *Journal of Psychological Researches*; 34(2); pp. 88-92.

Ara, Shabeen. (1995): Old age Homes: The Last Resort. *Research and Development Journal*; 2(1); pp. 3-10.

Arora, P.N. and Saxena, Shalini. (1997): A Study of Pattern of Adjustment of Retired Working and Non-Working Women in M.G. Husain (ed.); *Changing Indian Society and Status of Aged* New Delhi; Manak Publication.

Asha, C.B. and Subrahmanian, K.A. (1990): Problems of Elderly Women, Indian *Journal of Community Guidance Service*, Vol. 7, No. 3, pp. 61-67.

Bagchi, Kalyan (1997): The Plight of Elderly Females in India. In Bagchi, Kalyan (Ed.): *Elderly Females in India: Their Status and Suffering,* New Delhi: Society for Gerontological Research and Helpage India, pp. 11-22.

Bagga, Amrita. (1994) Health Status of Women in Old Age Homes. *Ageing and Society: The Indian Journal of Gerontology*; 4(3and 4); pp. 11-21.

Bali, Arun P. (1995): Role of the Family in Elderly Care, *Research and Development Journal*, Vol. 2, No. 1, pp. 30-40.

Bali, Arun P. (1995): Role of the Family in Elderly Care. *Research and Development Journal*; 2(1); Oct; pp. 30-40.

Bali, Arun P. (1995): Status of Gerontology and Geriatric Research in India: An overview and Guidance for further Research, *Research and Development Journal*, Vol. 1, No. 2, pp. 17-29.

Bambawale, Usha. (1997): The Abused Elderly. *Indian Journal of Medical Research;* 106; Oct; pp. 389-395.

Banerjee, Mrinmayi. (1997): Level of Isolation and Interpersonal Relationship of Aged Person in the Family: A Study in Shillong. *Ageing and Society: The Indian Journal of Gerontology*; 7 (3 and 4).

Bhatia, H.S. (1983): *Aging and Society: A Sociological Study of the Retired Public Servants,* Udaipur: The Arya Book Center Publishers.

Bhogle, S. and Reddy, R. (1996): Depression and Family Jointedness among Aged. In Kumar,Vinod (Ed.): *Aging: Indian Perspective and Global Scenario*. New Delhi: All India Institute of Medical Sciences, pp. 178-181.

Binstock R.H. and Shanas, E. (1976): *Handbook of Aging and Social Sciences*, New York: Van Nostrand Reinhold Company.

Birren, J.E., Woods, A.M. and Williams, M.V. (1980): Behaviour Showing with Age: Causes, Organization and Consequences. In Poon, L.W. (Ed.): *Aging in the 1980's: Psychological Issues*, Washington, D.C.: American Psychological Association.

Biswas, S.K. (1994): Implications of Population Ageing in India. In Ramchandran, C.R. and Shah, Bela (Eds.): *Public Health Implications of Aging in India*, New Delhi: Indian Council of Medical Research, pp. 22-35.

Blau, Zena Smith (1961): Structural Constraints on Friendships in Old Age, *American Sociological Review*, Vol. 26, No. 2, pp. 429-439.

Bose, A.B. and Gangrede, K.D. (Eds.), (1988): *The Aging in India: Problems and Potentialities*, New Delhi: Abhinav Publications.

Bose, Ashish (1996): *India's Basic Demographic Statistics*, Delhi: B.R. Publishing Corporations.

Bose, Ashish (1998): *Demographic Diversity of India, 1991 census, State and district level data supplement*, New Delhi: Ministry of Human Resources Development.

Bose, Ashish, (2000): Demographic Transition, *Seminar*, 488, April 2000, pp. 35-39.

Chadha, N.K. (1989): *Impact of Institutionalization on the Psychological Well-being and Depression among the Aged*, MS, National Symposium on Stress, Anxiety and Depression in Modern life, (Nov., 3-4, Patiala), Punjab University.

Chadha, N.K. (1991): Self-concept and Life-satisfaction among Aged, *Indian Journal of Gerontology,* Vol. 5, No. 1-2, pp. 47-54.

Chadha, N.K., Aggarwal, Vandana and Mangla A.P. (1992): Hopelessness, Alienation and Life–satisfaction among Aged, *Indian Journal of Gerontology,* Vol. 6., Nos. 3-4, pp. 82-92.

Chadha, N.K., Willigen, John Van and Kedia, Satish (1996): Late Life Changes in Social Networks and Disengagement: Perspectives from a Delhi Neighborhood, *Research and Development Journal*, Vol. 2, No. 3, pp. 7-15.

Chakravarty, Indrani (1996): Television and the Elderly: Indian Scenario. In Kumar, Vinod (ed): *Aging: Indian Perspective and Global Scenario*. New Delhi: All India Institute of Medical Sciences, pp. 235-236.

Chaney, E.M. (1990): Empowering Older Women: Evidence from Historical and Contemporary Sources. In Chaney, E.M. (Ed.): *Empowering Older Women*, Washington DC: AARP, pp. 5-11.

Chowdhry, D.P. (1992): *Aging and the Aged* (A Source Book), New Delhi: Inter India Publications.

D' Souza, Alfred (1982): *The Social Organization of Aging among the Urban Poor*, New Delhi: Indian Social Institute.

D' Souza, Victor S. (1990): The Simmering Problem of Aging in India: Some Emerging Issues, *BOLD Journal of the International Institute on Aging*, Vol. 4, No. 1, pp. 17-21.

Dak, T.M. and Sharma, M.L. (1987): Changing Status of the Aged in North Indian Villages. In Dak, T.M. and Sharma, M.L. (Eds.): *Aging in India*, New Delhi: Ajanta Publications.

Dandekar, Kumudini (1996): *The Elderly in India*, New Delhi: Sage Publications.

Das, Nimai Charam (1994): Psychology of Aging, *Journal of Community Guidance Research*, Vol. 11 (3), September, pp. 201-203.

De Alvarez, Julia Tavares (1991): Special Problems Facing Elderly Women in Developing Countries, *BOLD Journal of the International Institute on Aging*, Vol. 2, No. 1, pp. 2-4.

Desai, H.M. (1991): *Disabled Senior Citizens*, MS, WAB Workshop for the Blind, Bombay.

Desai, K.G. (1983): *Aging in India*, Bombay: Tata Institute of Social Sciences.

Desai, K.G. and Naik, R.D. (1970): *Problems of the Retired People in Greater Bombay*, Bombay: Tata Institute of Social Sciences.

Desai, Murli (1998): *Marginalization of Older Persons,* MS, Paper Presented at the National Conference on 21st Century: A New Environment for the Elderly, New Delhi, March 13-17, 1998.

Devi, Prasad (1997): *Elder Abuse and Neglect: A Review of Research and Programmes.* Paper presented at National Seminar on Globalisation and the Ageing: Implications for Gerontological Society Work.

Dhillon, Paramjeet Kaur (1992): *Psychosocial Aspects of Aging in India,* Concept Publication Company, New Delhi.

Dhillon, Paramjeet Kaur and Chhabra (1989): *The Coping Strategies of the Aged,* MS, Delhi University, Delhi.

Dhillon, Paramjeet Kaur and D'Sousa, Sheila (1992): The Effect of Age and Sex on Needs, Social Adjustment and Reactions to Frustration. In Dhillon, Paramjeet Kaur (Ed.):

Psychosocial *Aspects of Aging in India*, New Delhi, Concept Publication Company.

Duck, Steve (1986): *Human Relationships: An Introduction to Social Psychology*, New Delhi: Sage Publications.

Feinson, M. C. (1987): Mental Health and Aging: Are there Gender Differences? *The Gerontologist*, Vol. 27(1), pp. 303-311.

Ganesh Kamala (1997): Common Gynaecological Morbidity Pattern in Elderly Females. In Bagchi, Kalyan (Ed.): *Elderly Females in India*, New Delhi: Society for Gerontological Research and Helpage India, pp. 65-78.

Gangrede, K.D. (1989): Emerging Concept of Ageing in India: A Socio-cultural Perspective, *Eastern Anthropologist*, Vol. 42, No. 2, pp. 151- 169.

Gautam, Shiv and Pant, Anshuman (1997): Depressive Disorders in the Elderly, *Indian Journal of Gerontology*, Vol. 11, Nos. 3-4, pp. 52-67.

Getzen, Thomas E. (1992): Population Aging and the Growth of Health Expenditures, *Journal of Gerontology: Social Sciences*, Vol. 47, No. 3, S98-S104.

Government of India (1995): *The Country Paper For Beijing Conference*. Department of Women and Child Development, Ministry of Social Justice and Empowerment.

Government of India (1999): *National Policy on Older Persons*, Ministry of Social Justice and Empowerment, Shastri Bhawan, New Delhi.

Government of India (2002): *India 2002: A Reference*, New Delhi: Annual Publication Division, Ministry of Information and Broadcasting.

Grewal, Hirdaipal (1991): Lively and Cheerful, Though Retired, *Social Welfare*, Vol. XXXVII, No. 11-12, Feb.-March.

Guha Roy (2004): Demographic Aspects of elderly in India, In Ramamutri, P.V. and Jamuna, D. Ed. *Handbook of Indian Gerontology*, Delhi: Serial Publication.

Gupta HL, Yadav M, Sundarka MK, Talwar V, Saini M, Garg P. (2002): Study of Health Problems in Asymtomatic Elderly individuals in Delhi. *Journal of Association of Physicians in India* 2002; 50:792-5.

Gupta, P. and Vohra, A.K. (1987): Pattern of Psychiatric Morbidity in the Aged. In Dak, T.M. and Sharma, M.L. (Eds.): *Aging in India*, New Delhi: Ajanta Publications.

Gupta, S.P. (1993): Perspectives on the Sociology of Leisure : Reexamined, *Man in India*, Vol. 73, No. 3, pp. 315-320.

Hamilton, Ian Sturat, (1994): *The Psychology of Aging: An Introduction,* 2nd Edition, London: Jessica Kingsley Publishers.

Husain, M.G. (ed.). 1997. *Changing Indian Society and Status of Aged*. New Delhi; Manak Publications.

Jamuna, D. (1989a): Self-acceptance among Aged Women Belonging to Forward Class and Backward Class Groups, *Journal of Personality and Group Behaviour* Vol. 9(1), pp. 13-18.

Jamuna, D. (1989c): Psychological Problems and Perspectives of Aged Women. In Pati, R.N. and Jena, B. (Eds.): *Aged in India: Socio-demographic Dimensions*, New Delhi: Ashish Publishing House.

Jamuna, D. (1994): A Psychological and Social Correlates of Successful Aging among Elderly Indian Women, *Indian Journal of Gerontology*, Vol. 8, Nos. 1 and 2, pp. 18-23.

Jamuna, D. (1995): Ageing Women in India: A profile, *Research and development Journal,* Vol. 1(3), pp. 3-14.

Jamuna, D. and Reddy, N.K.L. (1991): The Widowed Rural Elderly: Status of Mental Health and Adjustment, *The Creative Psychologist* Vol. 3 (1), pp. 45-50.

Joseph, James (1991): *Aged in India: Problems and Personality*. Allahabad: Chugh Publications.

Joshi, P.C. and Sengupta, S.N. (2000): Health Issues, *Seminar,* Vol. 488, April, pp. 40-43.

Kailash, R.A. (1976): Death and Dying in Social Context. In Robert, B. and Shanas, Ethal, (Eds.): *Handbook of Aging and Social Sciences*, New York: Behavioural Publications, Inc.

Kakkar, Sudhir (1981): *The Inner World*, Delhi: Oxford University Press.

Kakkar, Sudhir (1982): *Identity and Adulthood,* Delhi: Oxford University Press.

Kamalamma, N. and Selsa, S. (2000): Urban Elderly Women: Problems and Solutions, *Social Welfare*, Vol. 47, June, pp. 30-33.

Kant, Anita and Sharma, Kavita (1996): Well-being and Aging: An Empirical Analysis, *Disabilities and Impairments*, 10 (2), pp. 101-110.

Kapur, Promila, (1997): Elderly Abuse: Some Counseling Tips. *Research and Development Journal*, Vol. 3, No. 3. pp. 13-23.

Kelvin Kinsella and Velkoff Victoria A (2000): An ageing World: *International Population Reports*, US Census Bureau and US National Institute of Ageing.

Khan, M. Z. (1997): *Elderly in Metropolis*. New Delhi: Inter-India Publications.

Khan, M.Z. and Bagley, N. (1989): Services for the Aged in India, In, Siddiqui, H.Y. (Ed.), *Social Welfare in India*, New Delhi: Harnam Publications.

Khan, M.Z. and Kaushik, Archana (1999): Where do the elderly stand in the changing economic scenario? *Social Welfare*, Vol. 46, No. 1, April, pp. 35-39.

Kirkwood, T.B.L. (1988): *The Nature and Cause of Aging. In Research and the Aging Population*, MS, CIBA Foundation Symposium, 134 Chichester: Wiley. 193-207.

Kohli, A.S. (1996): *Social Situation of the Aged in India*, New Delhi: Anmol Publications.

Krause, Neal (1997): Anticipated Support, Received Support and Economic Stress among Older Adults, *Journal of Gerontology- Psychological Sciences*, Vol. 52B, No. 6, pp. 284-293.

Kumar KV, Sivan YS, Reghu JR, Das R, Kutty VR. (1997): Health of the elderly in a community in transition: a survey inThiruvananthapuram City, Kerala, India. *International Journal on Aging and Human Development* 44:293-315.

Implications of Aging in India, New Delhi: Indian Council of Medical Research, pp. 99-105.

Prakash, Indira Jai (1996): Aging Women- A Liability or an Asset? *Research and Development Journal*, Vol. 2, No. 3, pp. 28-32.

Prakash, Indira Jai (1996): Coping with Aging: Psycho-social Situation of Older Indian Women. In Kumar, Vinod (Ed.): *Aging: Indian Perspective and Global Scenario*, New Delhi: All India Institute of Medical Sciences, pp. 291-293.

Prakash, Indira. Jai. (1989): *Life-cycle Changes in Aging Indian Women*, MS, Report submitted to UGC, New Delhi.

Prasad, P.H. (1990): Reservation and Class Structure of Castes, *Economic and Political Weekly*, Vol. 25, pp. 2.

Puri, Seema and Khanna, Kumud (1999): Health and Nutrition Profile of Middle Class Elderly Women Living in New Delhi, *Research and Development Journal*, Vol. 5, No. 3. pp. 18-26.

R., Kamala and Bhingradiya, Punita (1997): An Intergenerational Study on the Situation of the Elderly in Rural Saurashtra, *Indian Journal of Gerontology*, Vol. 11, Nos. 3and 4, pp. 78-84.

Raj, B. and Prasad, B.G., (1971): A Study of Rural Aged Persons in Social Profile, *Indian Journal of Social Work*, Vol. 32, No. 2, pp. 23-35.

Ramachandran, C.R.(1994): Introduction: The Emerging Problem of Old Age. In Ramchandran, C.R. and Shah, Bela (Eds.): *Public Health Implications of Aging in India*, New Delhi: Indian Council of Medical Research, pp. 2-3.

Ramamurti, P. V. (1970): Life-satisfaction in the Older Years, *Indian Journal of Gerontology*, Vol. 2, (3-4), pp. 68-70.

Ramamurti, P. V. (1972): *A Study of Role-availability, Role Utilization and Problems of Adjustment of Middle-aged and Older Individuals*, MS, Project Report, ICSSR, New Delhi.

Ramamurti, P. V. (1989): *An Empirical Study of Needs and Psychosocial Status of Widows of Weaker and Other Sections*, MS, Project Report, ICSSR, New Delhi.

Ramamurti, P.V. and Jamuna, D. (1986): *Self-other Perceptions of Issues and Problems of Aged Women in Andhra Pradesh, India*, MS, Abstracts of proceedings of IX World Congress of Sociology, ISA, New Delhi.

Ramamurti, P.V. and Jamuna, D. (1993a): Psychological Dimensions of Aging in India, *Indian Journal of Social Science*, Vol. 6(4), pp. 309-332.

Ramamurti, P.V., Jamuna, D. and Reddy, L.K. (1992b): Improving Human Resources among the Elderly — Effect of an Intervention, *Journal of Personality and Clinical Studies*, Vol. 8(1), pp. 77-79.

Randhawa, Maninder Singh, (1991): *The Rural and Urban Aged: A Sociological Perspective*, Patiala: National Book Organization.

Rao and Mahadevan (1983): *cited in* Ramamutri, P.V. and Jamuna, D. Ed. (2004) *Handbook of Indian Gerontology*, Delhi: Serial Publication.

Rao, P. Venkata (1994): Aging in Rural Society, *ICSSR Research Abstract Journal Quarterly*, Vol. XXIII, No. 1-2, Jan-June.

Rathore. Saroj. (1992): Subjective well-being in Old Age, *Indian Journal of Gerontology*, Vol. 6, Nos. 1 and 2. pp. 37-43.

Reddy, L. K. (1996): Health and Attitude Towards Health among Elderly. In Kumar, Vinod (Ed.): *Aging: Indian Perspective and Global Scenario*, New Delhi: All India Institute of Medical Sciences, pp. 231-234.

Registrar General and Census Commissioner (1992): *Ageing in India*: Paper No. 2 of 1992: India.

Registrar General, India (1997): *Census of India 1991, B series Economic Tables and C series Social and Cultural Tables*, New Delhi: Office of Registrar General of India.

Sahayam, M. Deva (1988): Aged Females: The Most Deprived Among the Deprived, *Indian Journal of Social Work*, Vol. 3, No. VIII, pp. 261-670.

Saroja, K. and Badiger, M.S. (1999): Case Study Approach for Research of Divorce, *Social Welfare*, Vol. 45, No. 11, pp. 26-29.

Vijayanunni, M. (1997): The Graying Population in India: 1991 Census Results, *Research and Development Journal*, Vol. 3, No. 3, pp. 3-12.

Wallace, Paul (1999): Age Quake: Riding the Demographic Roller-coaster Shaking Business, *Finance and Our World*, London: Nicholas Brealey Publishing.

WHO, (1996): Global Burden of Disease and Injury. In Khan, Sameera's Article, Your Life-style is Killing You, *The Sunday Times of India, Review*, December 22.

WHO, (1999): Ageing: Exploding the Myths. In The Art of Growing Old Healthfully: The Times of India, 23rd, March.

Wolff, K. (1959): Group Psychotherapy with Geriatric Patients in a State Hospital Setting: Results of a Three Year Study, *Group psychotherapy*, Vol. 12, pp. 218-222.

World Bank (1993): *World Development Report 1993: Investing in Health*. New York: Oxford University Press.

World Bank (1994): *A New Agenda for Women's Health and Nutrition*. World Bank, Washington DC.

Yadava KN, Yadava SS, Vajpeyi DK. (1994): Study of aged population and associated health risks in rural India. *Health Policy Plan* 9:331-6.

Index

G

H

I